The Speakers Journey (Volume Two)

Amplifying Your Voice

The Speakers Index

by Sharon Brown

THE BOOK CHIEF
IGNITE YOUR WRITING

TABLE OF CONTENTS

DEDICATION

To everyone who has stepped out of their comfort zone,
faced their fears and grabbed every opportunity to share
their journey with those who need to hear it!

ACKNOWLEDGEMENTS

Thank you to all of the Contributing Authors who have taken the steps to share their stories and bring this book to life.

Anna Goodwin, Dave Williams, Elle Bright, Femke Williams, Kevin Harvey, Lisa Billingham, Jasmine Mbye, Martin Sharp, Melitta Campbell, Mila Johansen, Rita Preston, Sharon Brown, Tabby Kerwin

INTRODUCTION

The second volume of this book is just as impactful as the first with each Author opening their heart to share how their journey began and how it has evolved throughout time, since they took that first step.

Some people find their true calling and take to it like a duck to water. Others have to work harder to come out of their comfort zone and face their fears.

We hope that by reading the stories within this book, it gives you, the reader, reassurance, motivation and confidence to face your own fears of public speaking.

If you're a business owner, you will have situations where you will need to speak up and speak out. There are many organisations that offer training and guidance on how you can build your confidence in this area and hone your skills to really complement and align with your business.

We at The Speakers Index support you in showcasing your skills through our directory and Speakers magazine and we encourage you to push yourself out there.

CHAPTER 1

Speaking from the Heart

By Anna Goodwin

Speaking has always been important to me. I've always been fascinated with people and being able to communicate with a room of people gives me joy. I don't remember a time when this wasn't the case.

When I was at Chuckery school from 8 to 10 years old, it was all about achieving in school, and of course, once you have this as an end game, you also have to have losers.

In many ways, I was bright and enjoyed schoolwork but struggled with maths, particularly with the maths teacher. Also, I couldn't pronounce my 'H's' and living in France as a child probably exacerbated this. Children love to ridicule, so each time I read aloud in class and mispronounced anything, I was laughed at.

To an extent, this discouraged me from wanting to read, but I still enjoyed it. To add to my isolation, I didn't like playtimes as I felt separate from everyone else, but I did enjoy giving the poorer children "Whizzers" (a type of spinning top). I didn't want them to feel left out, to feel like the underdog, as I frequently did.

I suppose the first time I spoke in public was a French-speaking competition – I know, listen to me! I read out the nursery rhyme Humpty Dumpty in French.

Before attending the event, I had practised and thought it came over well, but when I was there, I realised that some of the private schools' pupils had spent much longer practising and therefore gave a more polished performance. Our school didn't win, but even so, I enjoyed the experience, and it lit a fire within me!

While studying for my degree at Wolverhampton University, I always spoke up if I could see that people were struggling and getting left behind. I could empathise with them, as starting a one-year course in Financial Accounting after studying French, German, and English 'A' levels had been a shock to the system. Not surprisingly, I became the Student Representative, which meant I passed on any student concerns. I am always happy in this kind of role as I want to fight for the underdog, and I'm not afraid of speaking out. Of course, this communication was two-way – my fellow students needed to feel that they could approach me with their concerns and that I would listen and ask the right questions to get to the bottom of their concerns. Also, I had to translate their issues for the staff at the university.

From 1998 onwards, I worked in London for six-and-a-half years. My role was to audit universities and the Chamber of Commerce in France. This improved my speaking, and I learnt to think on my feet as I spoke in French. Also, I learnt to remain calm and in control; having 11 French people wanting to speak at once will do that! However, I relished the challenge.

I was a Woman in Rural Enterprise (WIRE) leader for four years. This entailed me running a monthly group for businesswomen. I started with four people; when I finished, there were twenty to twenty-five regular attendees. Not bad growth! This time taught me a lot about speaking as I learnt more about people; the audience is key.

Every event was organised using the same format and communicated to the speakers and the audience so they knew what to expect. By doing this, people knew the start and finish times and that these would be adhered to. It puts an audience at ease if they see the event is well-controlled.

There's nothing worse than being in an audience and wondering, 'How much longer is this going on for?' or worrying that you are going to miss your next appointment or picking the children up from school because the event is running over.

We started each session by going around the room and delivering our 60-second introductions. My favourite saying was, "Don't drone on"; I meant this in the nicest possible way, honest! Many people believe that saying more is better, but it isn't. If you go on too long, the audience loses focus, and your key message is lost.

It was a great experience running this group, and it improved my speaking ability as I was the one who always made the introductions and facilitated the meeting. Furthermore, I had to ensure the audience remained engaged, despite the variable quality of speakers! Also, I believe that small business owners developed their confidence in this supportive environment.

My communication skills were stretched a bit when in August 2014, I self-published my first book; Accountants *Don't Bite*. I dedicated this book to my friend Ruth Douglas who had died of cancer the year before. Turning to the written word as a main form of communication had many similarities to public speaking, but also, there is no 'live' audience for you to judge how your words are being received!

I held the book launch at the Hawkesyard Estate. What a great day! I spoke on the launch day, remembering my friend and feeling sheer enjoyment during the day. I suppose I thought that I had honoured her memory. It always helps when there is passion in what you speak about, as that will come across in how you talk. My book launch day was a prime example!

The following year I held my first Empowerment event raising money for Compton Hospice, where Ruth had died. Her final text to me was when she arrived there, and she said, "This place is awesome", so the hospice holds a special place in my heart. I wanted the event to be an opportunity to network, shop, learn, and raise money. Again, it was a wonderful day and another opportunity to speak and learn from speaking!

Again, I led the day's events and introduced each guest speaker and again, the day's purpose helped ensure that the speakers spoke from their hearts with passion.

I was accepted as a member of the Professional Speaking Association (PSA) in 2015. This felt like a great achievement as the level of speaking at the PSA is very high. I had to pinch myself that I was now part of such an elite group. Being part of this group helped and continues to allow me to improve my speaking. Their motto is "Speak more, speak better". That is true, as by taking as many speaking opportunities as possible, you learn more about how to be your speaking best. I know for some (many?), it can be a daunting prospect, but believe me, there is nothing like throwing yourself in at the deep end to gain experience. So, next time you are invited to speak, don't let the fear take hold; say YES!

At one of the PSA meetings, I had taken the 20-minute slot. For the first time, I'd decided to speak about my maths difficulties and my primary school maths teacher.

I'd always thought I couldn't share this as it would affect how people saw me as an accountant. But then I thought it was time to be my authentic self. After I finished, one of the speakers approached me and said that my talk had impacted her. She has always had a number block but hearing me speak and knowing that even with this unfortunate start, I have managed to be an accountant gave her confidence and hope. I felt privileged to have been able to help her and change how she feels about figures moving forward. It's a great feeling helping people to learn and get past their blocks, isn't it?! In doing so, I suppose I had gotten over one of my blocks too!

If I can use props when I speak, then I do! It breaks it up for the audience, and I love them too! Especially my coin sorter – it helps to get my points across, and what a crowd-pleaser! I learnt years ago there needs to be a reason why props are used and it's possible to overdo it; much better to have a few props that add to your presentation rather than too many. That goes for PowerPoint slides too! As an accountant, believe me, I have endured lots of terribly boring PowerPoint presentations over the years.

I aim to get the salient points across any slide deck and break them up with pictures. Just because you're learning a possibly dry topic doesn't mean it can't be fun! Please, don't just write everything you will say on your slides. Don't do it!

I am lucky to have had David Hyner as my mentor throughout my speaking career. It is so helpful to have someone in your corner; I can't recommend it enough. I always know that if I need to run something past him or ask him any queries, he is always there for me. Also, I have watched David speak many times, and each time I do, I learn something. He is always aware that the audience is essential, not him.

Even if you don't have a mentor, take particular notice when people speak – good and bad. Note what they do well and poorly and learn from them.

The Pandemic changed speaking events as they moved online. It is convenient to speak and train online, but I find it very tiring – for both the speaker and the audience. Also, it isn't easy to feel how your audience receives the information. Are they happy or thinking, "Beam me up, Scotty"? Also, it doesn't create the same energy as when you're face to face. For me, it's more challenging as I struggle with my hearing. Hence, having a group of people ask questions online is difficult. I find it helpful to engage the audience by asking questions and getting them to type comments for me to respond to. It still is nowhere near as effective as being in the same room, but it somehow keeps their interest – and mine!

Earlier last year, I spoke at the Pro Mobile Conference. I felt very honoured to have been asked as it's an important event for the DJs. One thing I noticed, not surprisingly, is that DJs are happy to interact and ask questions. Another reminder of how important it is to know your audience. I can assure you a group of accountants don't act the same way!

I had two workshops and one speaking session on the main stage during the weekend. The workshops were well attended, and everyone gained a lot from them. The main stage presentation was harder work. Before my moment, I had been watching the other presenters. When it came to questions, the presenter asked the audience, and they shouted their response. I told the organiser, "This doesn't work for me."

He said why didn't you say? I could have set the stage up differently so the audience's voices would be carried back to you. This reminded me to always speak to the organiser before an event!

I loved being on stage and the buzz of presenting to DJs who were interested in learning. In this instance, I had to walk to the edge of the stage to try and hear better. Forward planning next time!

I have learnt a lot as a speaker, and here are some tips to improve your speaking:

Practice, Practice, Practice

Any opportunity you have to improve your speaking, then go for it. Remember, initially, you'll probably be doing this free of charge. The experience is worth it, but financially, you won't be able to continue to work like this. At some point, you'll need to start charging.

Pricing

When you are asked what you charge, be careful to take account of your time. This includes preparation, delivery, travel time and costs. Also, value yourself – you may find your subject easy to understand, but it will take time to get to this level. Remember to charge for this!

Preparation

Please speak to the organiser and find out as much as possible about the audience, the venue, and the presentation they want you to give.

Go prepared with <u>anything</u> you might need. David Hyner takes a big suitcase to all his gigs, so he is ready and has items that the organiser or venue may need.

I take my clicker for my slides, books and business cards, laptop, food and drink, slides on my laptop and a USB, clipboard and paper, pens, banners etc.

Remember to practice your presentation repeatedly so that you don't need any script, and if someone asks you a question, you can quickly return to the point where you left your presentation.

Audience

Know your audience. For me, it's always helpful to know whether they're Directors or Sole Traders. What's important to them? What questions do they need to be answered by your presentation? You can even ask questions beforehand to give you time to prepare.

Please ensure they are comfortable and can see and hear your delivery.

Stories

Make sure you include stories when you present. If they're funny, even better, but they don't have to be. The aim is to be able to explain a point by using a story.

Everyone loves a story - I certainly do! But don't ramble on too much; otherwise, you'll lose your audience.

Props

Use these if you're drawn to them.

You need to be at ease when you present, so if using props doesn't work for you, don't use them! Make sure you have a reason for using them like my coin sorter mentioned earlier.

Takeaways

Think about which resources would be helpful for attendees. If you think about this as you are preparing your presentation, it will help to focus you. Remember, this is all about your audience, <u>not</u> you. Depending on my presentation, I might have a resources pack including a budget template, allowable expenses, and a one-page business plan template.

It always feels like an honour to be asked to speak, so I put the time in before an event to ensure everything flows well. It's worth it!

I hope you enjoy your speakers' journey. You'll learn a lot as you go, but if you keep learning, this will help you as a speaker. Ask questions as you go of the people you consider to be good speakers. If public speaking still terrifies you, maybe consider changing your thinking – by NOT speaking, you are depriving your future audience of new knowledge. Good Luck.

CHAPTER 2

Building Confidence

By Dave Williams

My speaking journey, like yours, started when I was a child, and I started sharing my first words, mum/dad or whatever my first words were. It has progressed substantially since then.

Most people get anxious and nervous when they feel they will have to speak in public when the reality is they have been doing it all their life. Think about it, when you are with a bunch of friends and you 'are holding court' sharing a story, you are speaking to an audience, so you are already an expert at public speaking.

My first experience speaking in front of a real group was when I was in school many years ago. It was only in front of the class, and I guess I was about 20 or so, and of course, at that time, the most important thing was to look good in front of my peers, so I didn't take things too seriously. I have always been a passionate, expressive speaker with many arm movements. At the time, my arms moved so much; I was like a portable air conditioning unit as my arms created so much airflow it couldn't help but cause a draft! I knew this was an issue, so I got my friends to tie my hands together so I wouldn't blow my classmates to the back of the room. Seemed a good idea at the time, especially as they tied my hands behind my back. Picture this; I am standing at the front of the room, in front of my class peers, with my hands tied behind my back, talking to the room; then reality sinks in. I cannot turn the pages of my notes as I cannot reach them because my hands are behind my back. Not the most promising start to public speaking by any means.

My next experience of speaking was when I was working in management roles. I remember being in front of the whole team when I was an assistant manager in a retail store. It was my first team meeting at the store, and I can't remember how many staff were there now as it was many years ago. Bear in mind that the room was packed out. It went well, and as I finished my talk, I finished with the wonderful phrase, 'Do it to them before they do it to you.' A lesson in how to lose the room quickly…and I have no idea where that phrase came from. I can still see some faces staring back at me with quizzical expressions.

Learning: sometimes you will come out with comments and phrases and need help understanding the rhyme or reason why? You will be getting feedback all the time.

I hated public speaking then and would do everything possible to avoid speaking in front of a group. However, during that time, I was regularly delivering training to the teams and, realistically, had no idea what I was doing. I was just being the authentic me and sharing information that I knew, and because these trainings were structured, I knew the 'audience' needed to know.

After joining an International Networking Organisation, my public speaking exposure increased dramatically. I had the opportunity to train at the monthly training and was very apprehensive.

On reflection, I was really poor when I first started this journey. However, they weren't looking for perfection, just people who had been through their journey to get there. I was so conscious that I couldn't recognise myself while delivering at the front of the room. It was like being on the side of a stage and watching myself from behind a curtain, thinking, 'Who's that?' An alter ego if you like.

However, I improved as my confidence increased, I took over these monthly meetings speaking at every event, and my confidence soared. I delivered more confidently, enjoying it more and finding my style. This led to delivering for the same organisation at the National Motorcycle Museum in front of about 1000 people. I was then asked to be MC with another organisation and provide training.

Has there still been cringe moments? That is the thing, life happens, and all you can do is your best even when' curveballs' come along out of your control.

Another cringe moment was when I worked for a banking organisation's division. I was training staff with a colleague, and all attendees were ladies. The training was going great.

Have you ever been in a situation where you have heard yourself saying something and questioned whether you said it or not? Well, that was me, I was talking about the impact on customers and how to serve them best, and unfortunately, I had a bit of a slip-up. Instead of saying customers, I replaced one of the 's' letters with an 'n'. I have no idea where that came from, as it isn't a word I have ever used. Imagine this, standing at the front of a room with delegates in front of you, and I was unsure if I had used the word until I saw my colleague at the back of the room crying with laughter and rolling around in her chair.

Consequently, I then got the giggles and persevered and completed the session. Only to receive feedback later that "it was the best training they had experienced." Learning: We are all human and should keep going.

Some years later, I was helping another organisation out with a training contract to help unemployed people get back into work. They were two-week courses about a particular subject and incorporated a bit of CV work so they could get interviews in the second week of the course. It was rather intense, and I pre-judged my audience. I had gotten caught up in the media blurb that unemployed people didn't want to work. How wrong I was. Everyone, and I mean everyone I had the pleasure of meeting, was brilliant, and all wanted to move forward. Note – don't pre-judge your audience. The format was a two-week course on a subject with some associated CV work.

After the first couple of days, what the delegates needed became apparent, so I changed the format – rebel that I am. Therefore, I changed the format to week one course training and week two into job preparation work, CVs, interview skills and motivating them to be their best selves. I am proud to say I was told I had the best job offer rate' throughout the company. Why? I gauged the audience and gave them what they needed.

Some of the delegates also suggested I became a motivational speaker! I had no idea where my content came from as it flowed from the heart. The reason I share that is not to share the results, just the transition I had personally, from pre-judging the groups before I started, adapting to what the groups needed and seeing them grow as people. Because of that, they moved their lives forward and began to feel significant again. It taught me another important lesson: depending on your speaking, impact your audience with content that will help them and change their emotion. Your audience is the most crucial element of your speaking; it is about making a difference.

If you can change them emotionally, you can be more impactful than ever. My speaking journey has been anything but plain sailing, and I also run my live events. Even now, there are still hiccups. Most of the time, though, the audience doesn't typically realise.

However, let me take you back a few years. I was running a free event in Derby and had been promoting it like crazy and had a good number of people registered to attend the event. I had a helper who would sort registration and look after the guests when they arrived. An hour or so before the event started, I received a call to say my helper had been taken ill. Ok, so this is going to be a 'one-man band'.

I arrived at the venue, knowing that time would be of the essence, but I knew I had plenty of time to get everything sorted. Guess what? They can't find the keys to the room. Do you ever feel that things are destined to be a challenge?

They eventually found the keys; great, let's crack on. The venue had promoted they had all this top-notch audio-visual equipment. Brilliant, so my presentation was going to look professional. If only it were that simple! The machine they had wouldn't connect with my laptop, and it took up loads of time trying to resolve it. So as this was taking time, it took time away from my set-up time, and guests started arriving early.

When you usually want people to arrive early, something happens, and they arrive extra early! Yup, this happened, so I wasn't even set up, so it became a bit of a challenging night.

On reflection, I learned I had gotten everything sorted as much as I could have, and outside influences derailed the event's professionalism. I managed to impact the people there, which was what mattered. Things will happen beyond your control, and all you can do is adapt to the situation, which is what I did.

I was invited to another event as the Keynote speaker which was the second time I had spoken with this organisation. It was an honour to be asked to speak for them again, and always lovely to be re-booked. The brief I had was so open that I must admit, I found it challenging. It was to virtually talk about whatever I wanted with no guidance whatsoever. This is often the worst scenario. I have previously mentioned that knowing your audience is vital. I had spoken with the event planner – the drawback was there were two of them – and I made my request for a hands-free mic, and also guided them through how to do timings etc., as they hadn't planned that at all.

I got to the venue, and was looking forward to it. I met many of the hierarchy I had met at my previous engagement, and they even remembered me, which I was amazed about. Then I discovered there was no hands-free mic, only a handheld, which I found an issue because of my speaking style. Before I was about to go on for my slot, I was told they were running behind schedule, so could I reduce my timings? No problem, as there are always things I can introduce or drop, but I needed the timing cards to let me know where I was.

The music started, and everyone was getting engaged after a long day of other speakers who didn't engage with the audience. Great start, and then the system crashed, so my slides didn't work on their system. Ok, interesting, eh? Then I noticed I wasn't getting the time checks I needed, and I did check, and the event organiser had lost track of time, so I was talking 'blind'. Fortunately, I had practised like crazy and had a rough idea of where I was, but as I was asked to reduce my timings, I was now unsure. I must admit, after completing my keynote slot, I was feeling a little deflated because it didn't go as well as I had anticipated because of the changes that were imposed, and then I received this message from one of the attendees:

"I must say I like what you do and how you take your audience on a thought-provoking journey of self-exploration and discovery. Very difficult to do what you do and do it well, which you did, where people left feeling empowered." - Ron Lawrence MBE.

I am forever in Ron's debt for his wonderful comments.

Here's the thing, it is not about us as speakers; it is about the audience and giving them what they need and doing it with congruency and passion.

Not long after that event, Covid happened, and most people were thrown into lockdowns. I had no idea how the speaking format would go – probably like most others. Then we hear of Zoom (other brands are available). Whereas I had thought speaking would be struggling, it has taken things to a different stratosphere. From those wonderful experiences throughout my speaking journey, the ups and downs, it has been an incredible journey that I cherish.

Since then, the virtual opportunities have been fantastic, and I have had the chance to speak in North America, South America, Mainland Europe, and Australia, impacting people along the way. Receiving feedback such as: *"Thank you, that was inspirational."*

"I enjoyed it. I could relate to it and realised I never set goals anymore; I stay in my comfort zone. So, I realised that I needed to change and have set 5 goals to focus on, and I'm working through them, thanks to you."

"Thank you, that has given me the belief that I need to change and can change things for the better."

"Dave, it was an immensely enlightening experience. Just what I needed at my lowest ebb. Thank you SO VERY MUCH for this experience."

"Just a quick note to thank you for all your help and assistance yesterday. Several lightbulb moments during the day will see a massive change in my approach. Over time, I have built some blockers up that meant I could not see the woods for the trees."

"Without hesitation, you've been the best guest speaker we have ever had."

Now, I have not shared these testimonials to say, "Aren't I good" or anything like that – quite the opposite, in all honesty. I have shared many of my ups and downs, and the thing is, when you speak, you will get better, although ultimately, speaking is not about you or me. It is about your audience and who you can help to change, inspire, and make a difference to.

Share your message, and you don't know who you will impact positively and maybe, even change their lives for the better. When you serve people, many opportunities can open up for you. I have had the pleasure of being recommended to other organisations as a speaker. If I can achieve this, with my ups and downs, you can achieve whatever you want and use my experiences to laugh at and learn from.

To your success!

Dave

CHAPTER 3

How to Step into the Power of Speaking

By Elle Bright

The truth is that we all have something worth saying; although you may not believe it…yet.

We all have individual experiences of the world and each other, and no one else can make the same contribution as you can. We all have the capacity to help one another if we so choose and becoming a Speaker, whether that's a large or small part of who you are, is your choice.

In today's technology, almost everyone has access to the internet and the ability to broadcast whatever they think and feel live to millions. But once it's "out there", you can't easily, if ever successfully, remove it, and that is one reason so many people are scared to be seen and heard, to speak up, to speak their truth or even the truth of others, to become a Speaker.

And for everyone I've ever met or studied who has used their voice publicly, there's been a journey, sometimes a hero's journey overcoming all the odds to become a Speaker.

My journey may or may not resonate with you, but I'm sure you can take something of value from it. At least, I hope so!

So here it is!

I remember being quiet at school, trying to be the teacher's pet to avoid detention but also trying not to stand out as much as I didn't want to be bullied (who does?). This exemplifies what we all want to achieve in life, work, and business – be seen, heard, and accepted for who we are and our unique values but not be rejected, bullied, made fun of, or criticised. It's a delicate balance, and it basically keeps you in a stuck place of never really being yourself or making that contribution for fear of retribution or rejection.

During my school years, I didn't show up or want to be heard at all except that I played in orchestras and bands and the rare solo, which did at least validate my ability to show up as me, even if that was only amongst "music types" with whom I "belonged". There was no speaking whatsoever unless, when necessary, a quiet "thankyou"!

When it came to further education, there was no expectation from my family that I would go to university, but I got great national results, applied and got in.

I was the first of my family since my father to go to university, and he had failed his first year because he didn't even attend lectures. Naive in what I wanted to do and who I wanted to become, I tried to keep my study as broad as possible but wanted to come out of it with the best chance of getting a good stable job! Again, the push and pull of being you but not being rejected!

So, I began a law degree but wanted to do science as well because I loved science, and I had missed out on being accepted into the double degree which was being offered for the first time that year in my state because my grades weren't high enough.

I quickly realised that I was amongst extremely intelligent and very capable students. My previous strategy of laying low wasn't going to cut it for me to excel, but, in my mind, to make laying low my desired result, I determined that I'd be best placed to become a solicitor, the type of lawyer who works in the back room, and not a barrister who was the one who stood up and spoke in court.

This is the sort of fantastical "justification wriggle" that our minds do every day to keep us stuck and safe!

My law degree studies included lectures with hundreds of students and study groups, and I did my best to push myself to participate in those because I couldn't ask or answer a question in lectures in front of all those people to save my life! In study groups, we had to stand up and give full answers and sometimes a presentation of up to 15 minutes. We were graded on these, and it was torture. However, wanting to succeed in becoming a backroom solicitor, I did it through willpower, and the positive feedback I received helped me gain confidence.

Remembering my love of science, I spring boarded off my good grades and fresh confidence.

I made an appointment with the Dean of the Law Faculty to request that my elective subjects be science because I had wanted to do a double degree. The university where I was enrolled didn't offer a double degree yet, which interested them in my proposition. My request was granted on the basis that I was to be assessed every semester, and my experiment would be stopped if my law grades weren't good enough. This threat ensured that I worked hard, and at the end of the semester, before the results were out, the Dean's office called me and requested a meeting the next day.

I'm sure you can imagine the extreme visceral fear that shot up inside me! It turned out that I'd done so well in my first science subjects that they wanted to know if I wished to continue and essentially complete the two degrees in tandem. I agreed in a haze of excitement and fear and the terms of our agreement were that I had to complete all of the degree requirements, and my progress would continue to be assessed and approved or disapproved every semester. I'd only receive any special consideration if two exams or lectures that required my attendance were on at precisely the same time.

So what's this got to do with becoming a Speaker?

Well, from my experience, research and study of Speakers, I have found that to be a Speaker, you need to own that identity and to own it, you need to see it, acknowledge it, accept it, embody it and get enough positive confirming results from being it to continue! When we own it, it forms a part of our identity and this is how we create any permanent change in our identity.

To become a non-smoker, you have to own being a non-smoker and take action to not smoke.

To become a writer, you have to own being a writer and do what writers do, write! This is why speaking up for yourself (or others) is an important phase of the speaker's journey.

My experience of speaking up for myself and asking for what I wanted with positive results helped lay the foundation for my becoming a confident Speaker. Giving presentations and getting good grades installed that identity in my mind, and successfully completing the two degrees in five years reinforced my belief in my identity as a Speaker; it didn't matter that being a Speaker wasn't a large part. Once that identity is there, you can build on it.

This is why what I call "identity forensics" is powerful.

When a client is levelling up and wants to take on a new identity, whether that's a 7-figure earner, only working three days a week, or becoming a Writer or Speaker, we look in their timeline and notice all the evidence that proves that who they want to become is already a part of who they are now.

It's a beautiful realisation to discover and acknowledge defining moments that form the threads in your life that have constantly been weaving into your identity and to see that identity, acknowledge it, accept it, own it, embody it and be it.

I once had a client who had a court case coming up. She had been discriminated against in the workplace and dreaded speaking in court. She suffered from PTSD, but in just a few coaching sessions, we traced that thread and cleared the Imposter Syndrome blocks that were coming up in order to protect her but were preventing her from being able to speak, so she could own her identity and become a Speaker, "speaking her truth" in her court case only a few weeks later.

When you allow yourself to be who you truly are, changing who you define yourself as without trying to fix yourself into who you want to become, can happen quickly. It is with absolute joy that I get to see her continue to blossom into owning more and more of who she truly is.

You see, what I've discovered is that becoming a Speaker, or whoever you want to be, is all about your perception of your who you are and being a Speaker is not a natural identity for most of us.

Glossophobia, or the fear of public speaking, is a very common phobia that is believed to affect up to 75% of the population. It's easy to understand why we fear speaking up. We live in a structured society, albeit democratic, where one represents many.

Not everyone gets to speak, even though we all can and if you show up and speak in front of a group, you need to be calm and authoritative and prepared for questions, disagreement, criticism and conflict. It's a big responsibility.

Since we evolved from animals, we can also look to the animal kingdom and see that the animal that stands apart is the leader. The injured or rejected animal can easily end up as dinner for a predator!

We all know that a baby or toddler, if abandoned physically or by lack of love and belonging, has little chance of survival and we instinctually behave accordingly - our base motivation is to be safe and to belong. Scientists have shown that it's not until around seven years of age that our adult brain has formed.

Our brain (and some argue this applies to all of our cells) contains our interpretation or "coding" of everything we've experienced or been taught, along with our inherited DNA.

So, unless you have a genetic inheritance or have learnt that you are a leader or that being a Speaker is safe and right for you, you will be hardwired and encoded to instantly know and react to it being completely unsafe.

Your instincts will be telling you to keep with the group, especially your family – physically, mentally, emotionally – and not to stray or speak up or be different because that's unsafe and that rejection can lead to death.

This makes it perfectly logical that even the thought of public speaking can cause full-on panic and fear. Even though physical death is extremely unlikely today for most people (unless you live in some god-awful place in the world), it can certainly feel like it. The threat of psychological death, for your thoughts or emotions to be rejected, is real; in our mind, it's tantamount to physical rejection, abandonment and imminent demise.

That is how powerful our mind is. That is how perfectly programmed our minds can be. That is why we stay in our comfort zone. Outside is unsafe and unknown, and you won't belong anymore. But our brain doesn't stop forming at seven years of age.

We now have scientific proof that new brain cells can form throughout our lives and allow our minds to be programmed differently at any time.

We all know that we can learn new habits, you can recover from a brain injury and can be released from phobias like public speaking.

We can change our minds! So, maybe you were born with the fear of public speaking, but change is possible and inevitable if you want it to be. Our minds are more powerful than we'd ever thought.

And how do you change your perception of your identity? There are three ways, and we've already spoken of two. The first is to build the habit, train, and practise so that, eventually, the identity is "real". The second is to experience a significant event and interpret that as making that change in your identity.

The third is to never forget that how you interpret everything is up to you. You could be in an accident and be in a wheelchair from then on. You could use this to become a victim or decide to empower others who, like you, are in a wheelchair. You choose.

So when you decide to be a Speaker, you live the life of a Speaker; you take actions aligned with that identity.

However, you define it and in whatever proportion you decide, you support that to the best of your ability with training, practice, and significant experiences. After all, it's your perception, your concept of who you are, and you clear and release any resistance that comes up when you want to train, practice, embody, and believe in your new identity.

I call the resistance, Imposter Syndrome blocks, and I help women entrepreneurs systematically rewire and recode their thoughts and feelings to help those blocks dissolve. You've gained them from your ancestors or your personal experiences or the thoughts and feelings of others, but you get the final say on who you are, no one else.

There's nothing wrong with you; you aren't incapable of becoming a Speaker even if you have no voice; technology will help you (!); you aren't unworthy because everyone has an individual experience and vision, and so sharing that and connecting can only make the lives of every one of us even richer.

So, you might have guessed by now that after completing my double degree, I worked in science, and you'd be right! But I didn't get a degree in biology, neuroscience, or even biochemistry, but the chemistry of gold!

I believe that my work in science – often as the only woman at the table with millionaires or the boss of hundreds of men in a remote part of the world – helped me to challenge myself in terms of showing up and being seen and heard.

Being quiet wasn't an option. In fact, in 2005, during my PhD studies, I won "Best Student Presentation" at an international geological conference in China. I presented my research to nearly 500 peers in an auditorium in Beijing. I feel that winning that award cemented an unshakeable belief in myself, not only as a Speaker.

Now, before a speaking event or a photo shoot, I get to experience nervous excitement because I've rewired and recoded my thoughts and feelings to love public speaking! And presentations don't always go 100% to plan.

I once turned up to give a talk on photography, and there wasn't a screen or projector or any way to show my PowerPoint of gorgeous images, and I didn't have physical samples either! And there are times when the mic didn't work, the digital slides somehow went haywire, or there were disruptive sounds from outside or a heckler in the audience!

The key to it all is to own it and step into the power of your truth. There's no need to be an imposter.

You can rewire and recode your thoughts and emotions and become who you want to be. You can ignore any mistakes you make (it's not like the audience knows most of the time anyway!), or you can address them and incorporate them into the conversation. It doesn't matter. What truly matters is to communicate to the best of your ability in the circumstances and speak your truth so that you can reach out and connect with your listener, and they can, in turn, connect with you.

That synergy is a beautiful thing! It can, through speaking and connection, change the world. Many great Speakers already have.

For me, weaving those threads together, I re-became a Speaker after my first career, in gold exploration and investment, and my second career, photography, because my incredible boudoir clients created the need in me to research, study and train in developing a system to create confidence and become who we want to be.

How?

My clients would arrive at my studio a bundle of nerves, almost scared to death, and after their photoshoot, even if they hadn't seen their images yet, they would leave like a lioness full of confidence.

And not only that, they would go and take action to change their lives for the better! Women left abusive husbands, booked those trips to where they'd always wanted to go, aced that job interview, changed careers, and more!

And their photos took on the role of the physical proof of their confidence transformation. They were so much more than pictures. There were so many women who positively changed the trajectory of their lives for the better that the scientist in me had to solve the puzzle! Long story cut short, I figured it out, and that's what I do now – I help women women entrepreneurs overcome Imposter Syndrome and bring the power of their truth to the world through speaking, writing, showing up and being seen and heard.

And I love to speak all about it! Because I believe the more women who speak up, the more women will feel that they can too, and all of these fantastic individual contributions will make the world a better place, just because you and me and all of us, every one of us, speak our truth.

CHAPTER 4

A Journey of the Soul

By Femke Williams

"Where's she gone now?"

As a child, I was often 'away with the fairies', as my parents used to tell me. They would have taken their eyes off me for a second, and I was gone! So, they would joke I had been taken by the fairies.

In a way, they were not wrong. I was happiest outside, in my own company, in a tree, or sitting for hours by a molehill at twilight to catch the little creature when it would come out! I would then bring it over to anyone who wanted to see so I could share this wonder.

Another time I would have been playing outside and going into someone else's house without telling my parents. I am pretty sure most kids will have done this at some point! As an 80s child, I think we were left to explore that little bit more, not carrying a phone and parents/carers trusting that their kids were safe.

51

It may also have something to do with the fact that I was born and bred in The Netherlands – perhaps the approach to upbringing there is slightly more 'free' and less prudish than in the UK. (or at least I believe it was back then!)

Either way, I would always come back with stories. After having told me off for disappearing, I'm grateful that my parents did take the time to listen. They encouraged my brother and me to explore, connect with nature, and have fun as much as possible.

I also used to journal about my experiences, especially how they had made me feel, good or bad, and I would make plenty of drawings of the animals I'd seen or what had inspired me, with colour and shapes. That was another way of sharing what was going on for me and anchoring my experiences (although I didn't realise back then that's what I was doing).

Becoming who I am

My speaking journey started with comfortably sharing with others about my experiences and trusting that they had time for me. I know that this had a positive impact on me and on those who listened and cared.

At school, I got involved with organising and creating artwork for events and various theatre plays, and I was often chosen to guide newbies around the school. I was lucky that my teachers were very observant and helped their students develop their natural skills.

As a teenager, I became more aware of the things that we didn't have, as opposed to what we did and should be grateful for. I rebelled a little against my mum as she was always so over-giving, at massive personal cost. She had time for everyone else; the house almost always had a visitor when I'd return from school, or she'd be helping out someone somewhere. There was no time for me, and she no longer listened to my stories. At least, that's how I viewed it, and I despised that she never said 'no' to others and how they had certain expectations of her. I felt she ignored what was important, and I could also see it affected her health negatively.

It motivated me to start a career in healthcare, to help 'fix' her and others. Deep down, I was looking for more natural ways to healing and well-being, but of course, 'career guidance' would not recommend anything that wasn't backed up by science and 'doing reflexology' would not pay the bills!

So, I took up four years of Nursing College, which in the third year opened up an opportunity to gain hospital experience as a student nurse in a country abroad, including developing countries. A fellow student and I arranged for this to happen for us, and we travelled to Cameroon, where we spent about four months working in a Mission Hospital.

I felt truly at ease there; I don't know what it was, but the whole environment, the people, and their approach to life and health.

I helped to run the Mother and Child clinics, delivering talks around primary health care topics and travelling to other communities to do the same. Always working with what we had. This was such an eye-opener for me.

I realised at home I had adopted a lack-mentality, meaning I believed there was never enough to be happy; not enough time, not enough money, not enough love, not enough attention, just not enough anything. Even myself being 'not enough'. I could now see that this was just a 'belief'. I was telling myself this. In Africa, within the hospital, we worked with what we had, and yes, this was tough at times. But as a community, we were always looking for solutions instead of continuously complaining and highlighting the problem.

Here, I learned to accept 'what is'. To be content with what we have in the present moment. Gratitude.

Back in the Netherlands, it led me to study Health Education and Promotion at UNI (MSc), believing I could then better share positive health messages with the wider community around preventing, intercepting and recovering from disease.

Another opportunity to go abroad for my research implementation and evaluation came along, and I went to South America (British Guyana), this time for seven months, on my own. I implemented a Primary Health Care Programme developed by UNESCO, WHO & UNICEF within primary schools and a couple of secondary schools.

What an amazing experience! There, I aspired to integrate everything I had learned so far and my natural talents into a way of sharing the various' facts for life' topics with the children and teachers in such a way that they were fully engaged and would learn the core messages through song, art and dramatics. The children then performed for their parents and the wider community and displayed their artwork during a festival day that brought it all together.

I was actually doing and organising all this, getting local sponsors and all sorts of support for the festival day, but I was totally in my flow. I LOVED doing this. I saw the impact it had on all involved. I made so many amazing connections. I was interviewed on the radio, which was broadcast all over Guyana.

As I travelled the country during the last few weeks there, I met people who had heard me speak on the radio, and they told me what it meant to them, what they'd learned from it, and how they were passing it on to their families. Amazing.

However, as I returned home, I was overwhelmed with all of the experiences and wondered what the heck I was going to do next. I also had found deep love with someone over there, and as I left it all behind, my heart was breaking while we tried; things seemed too complicated for us to keep our relationship going.

After graduating, I had to choose whether to return for three years to help implement the programme in other areas or start my career in the Netherlands.

The Shift

Somehow, I was completely exhausted after my return, and I repressed strong emotions, telling myself to get on with it, to let go, and look ahead for opportunities available to me now. I took the first job I was offered at the University Hospital as a Clinical Research Assistant and 'got on with it'.

Looking back, it was the start of my spiritual and healing journey. I've always felt that there is more between heaven and earth than the physical eyes can see or what we get taught within our modern society about what life is all about. I feel such a strong connection with the natural world, and it was a book (given to me by my mum) called '*The Camino – a Pilgrimage of Courage*' by Shirley MacLaine that nudged me to come back out of my shell and let nature and my Higher Self guide me! Because I realised, I was still exhausted and it was not something I wanted to 'normalise' being only 24. It was not right. Something was amiss. I needed to find within myself what I actually wanted to do next.

I felt I needed to reconnect with nature and my body and release the pain in my heavy heart. So, I went on a backpacking holiday in Scotland with a good friend because I wanted to walk, feel the earth under my feet, be higher up in the mountains so I could have a vision from above, and let the wind caress my hair... To just be present! To feel joyful again.

Funnily enough, my opening heart led me straight towards meeting my now husband, there, on Ben Nevis! I moved to Scotland five months later. My parents were supportive but must have just thought, 'Where's *she gone now?*' They had seen me go through all these recent motions, and here I was going on yet another adventure with a separated man who had two boys of 4 and 6.

To cut a very long story short, I had found new love and once again decided I had left certain things behind me. I just threw myself into this new life abroad, and my work saw me deliver training to groups and presenting within the field of Clinical Trial Research.

It was a great time for personal and professional development because it meant I had to improve my speaking skills. It took a great deal of courage to gather my nerves and talk about a holistic approach to clinical trial support if there was such a thing!

In training and presenting to larger groups, I shared my knowledge from the field of Nursing & Health Promotion (including Cognitive Behavioural Therapy strategies) to help trainees mentally and emotionally prepare for customer services and take calls for international clinical trial support and patient recruitment.

I reached a point of burnout twice within about five years because I was still physically and emotionally exhausted. My husband and I married and went on to have two more children, and I ignored all the little red flags. I told myself I should be happy with my lovely family and a good job, but I had suppressed crying, mood swings and digestive issues, and it started to have a very negative impact on my health and well-being. I had unexplained aches, pains and emotions, was intolerant to various painkillers and muscle relaxants, was so tired and felt like a shitty mother showing my emotions in front of the kids. I drank too much as a coping mechanism, believing it would help me to relax and be more mellow. I never abused alcohol but drank daily, and my body did not thank me for it.

On a Mother's Day Sunday, my day off from working nursing shifts around childcare, my husband brought our one and 3-year-old into the bedroom to wake me up with gifts & breakfast at 6:30 am.

I just broke down.

I will never forget the looks on my babies' faces . seeing mummy crying and turning away from them when they were there with gifts and love. Or the way that my husband reacted. It still makes me cry.

The guilt, shame and powerlessness I felt is indescribable.

But the experience was so powerful, and this had to happen for me to see that I needed to change things.

It was also when I realised that I had to do some soul work concerning unprocessed memories and unresolved issues from years ago. I had to dig deep, acknowledge and accept all of me, including my shadows, put that radical self-care in place, ask for support, forgive myself and others, and prioritise my health and well-being. On top of that, I could see the patterns of generational trauma within my family - how this has affected the women's physical and emotional health and that it is passed on if the cycle is not broken.

To help me overcome those deep feelings of sadness and loss, I asked for support, had holistic therapy, and brought back things I love doing into my life; dancing, music, drawing and painting. Surrounding myself with nature and good friends. Saying 'no' to other people, things and situations. Walking. All ways to freely express my feelings and to make time for my needs. Creating the shift.

Embodied Health

Once our kids were both at school, I decided to follow my dream of being a Reflexologist. I set up my business in 2012. It has now developed into Rosewood Wellbeing, where I am a sole trader and appoint myself as a Natural Healer, Intuitive Artist and Soul & Wellbeing Coach/Mentor.

Health is so much more than the absence of physical illness! It is everything we are through an embodied (holistic) approach; physical, emotional, mental, relational, environmental and spiritual.

During lockdown, my journey saw me studying well-being and Specialist Coaching with *The Chrysalis Effect Health* in supporting ME/Chronic Fatigue Syndrome and Fibromyalgia Recovery (including long-covid). I learned so much, realised only then what burnout really is and linked it back to the times I 'crashed', and I am convinced that my mum suffered from fibromyalgia but was never diagnosed.

I now know that it is possible to recover from these conditions fully, and I talk about the early warning signs, coping mechanisms, possible causes of extreme fatigue and the link between physical and emotional symptoms.

With awareness, time, investment, courage and commitment, my clients can prevent and intercept burnout as I did; they can work through traumas and recover from chronic exhaustive conditions.

They truly claim back their health, harmony and vitality and free their Wild Souls, and to see them flourish like that is the most rewarding thing ever!

I communicate the healing properties of energy, colour and the creative process through therapy, coaching / mentoring, art workshops and Chakra dance (moving meditation) and how these can help positively transform our lives. I have this deep desire to help others (re)connect to nature and themselves, cultivate self-love and embody all of who they are. I am passing on what I've learned, what I did, and how I've coped and flourished.

While everyone's healing journey is unique, it is about understanding our true values and creating inner calm and peace amidst the chaos. To become detached from patterns of behaviour and limiting beliefs that we bind ourselves to. We are all conditioned by our family lineage, our upbringing and our environment and experiences as to what we come to believe and how we are supposed to live our lives until we really come home to self and realise that we can live by our true values and beliefs, and create a life that we love.

Where I once uncomfortably trained and presented to groups about a holistic approach to Clinical Trial Research (I realise it didn't sit right with my values, and it drained me), I now talk to groups, networking communities and for The Chrysalis Effect Recovery Support, about my story and an embodied approach to overcoming *disease*.

I also interact through Facebook Lives and Zoom calls where people can relate and share their experiences, too, so we can all learn from each other.

Raising Vibration

I believe that through the Healing Arts (music, voice, sound, movement/dance, the intuitive body and Art), we can help bring that highest vibration – *Love* – back into our hearts when we feel we may have lost it.

Speaking to the public in the ways I do now has definitely changed me for the better; it has raised my confidence and my profile, but the best thing is that it makes such a difference to others. So many reach that point of near burnout but keep pushing past their limits until they crash and then don't understand why they have no energy for anything and become ill or even bedbound. When I explain how Chronic Fatigue Syndrome and Fibromyalgia can come about and how it is possible to recover from physical pain and emotional fatigue, emotions can run high with the realisation that they can get better. Those individuals drive me, resonate with me, and need to hear what I have to say.

With my inner child in mind, I passionately and creatively share my stories, experiences and ways of healing our lives. My followers, listeners and clients are becoming motivated and committed to creating positive change and health for themselves and their offspring. It has an impact, which is my WHY for doing what I do.

When we can individually heal from the inside out and raise our vibration by expressing ourselves freely, it creates a ripple effect on others, our direct environment and beyond.

'Where's *she gone now?*'

She's freeing her Wild Soul!

CHAPTER 5

Beyond Impressive

By Jasmine Mbye

I had recently spoken at the Global IFPI PRC Conference, which was held each year, and attended by the top music executives from countries around the world. (This was back when you flew around the world to attend meetings in person about 2008 or 2009). Not only had I been invited to share on this world platform, based on the training I delivered, but I had smashed it! Thankfully, I wasn't alone in thinking that I'd done a sterling job.

I received great feedback on the day and, the organisation I worked for at the time, received a number of emails speaking highly of my presentation.

One of the key music executives who attended described it as 'very impressive'. I was chuffed, as it's great when you think you do something well, but better when other people, whose opinions you value, agree.

It's often asked, "Are the greats made or are they born?" What do you think?

I'm unable to answer that as Bishop TD Jakes, who is an amazing world renown speaker and preacher, used to stutter.

What I do believe though, is that I was born to be a speaker! You see this wasn't the first time I had a great audience or received glowing feedback.

As a child I read at a Christingle service attended by Queen Elizabeth II. While at Sixth Form I delivered a presentation at the National Portrait Gallery and was told 'it was one of the best presentations ever', (and they'd seen a lot of presentations).

I was born to be a great speaker and thanks to Mrs Metcalf, I'd had lots of practice, so public speaking wasn't at all daunting for me.

I've always been quite chatty and would get told off in my infant class for talking. My classmates would be chatting away and I'd say one word like 'yeah' and my teacher would tell me off. I'd complain how unfair it was that my friends had been talking for ages and I say one word and get told off.

My teachers' response was always, 'Jasmine your voice carries'.

Thankfully, all it took to make a huge difference was one great teacher when I moved into junior school. Mrs Metcalf recognised that my love of talking and my voice that carried should be channelled.

I have been speaking publicly ever since…from 7 years of age.

Each class would take turns to do the year assembly. When it was our class' turn, I would have to read the story and was envious of my classmates who got to act out Roald Dahl, doing fun things like jumping on mats.

Now, I'm so grateful because little did I know how that set me up to be the speaker that I am today.

It's taken some time to consider myself a speaker. At the time I received that fabulous feedback regarding my speaker presentation at the Global IFPI PRC Conference, I didn't consider myself a speaker. I only considered myself a trainer, although I knew I could speak and would take opportunities to speak when presented to me, pretty much nailing it each time.

I still didn't consider myself a speaker because my mindset limited me to thinking I could only be one thing.

A few years prior, I had been given some great life advice at church; 'whatever you would do for free, that's what you should do for a living'. I thought, well I'll talk for free so I searched online for jobs where I get paid to talk. The first job that came up was a speaker. However, my instant thought was what have I got to say that someone's going to pay me to speak, so I dismissed it and thought I'll come back to that later.

Next on the list was a trainer, something which seemed more doable. I just needed to get qualified and could go from there. So I did just that. I undertook a CIPD (Chartered Institute of Personnel and Development) Certificate in Training Practice qualification. I was advised by a trainer I admired, that the training and development world is difficult to get into so it would be best to attempt that move in my current organisation. I had never been shy to go for what I wanted when it comes to work so I set to work getting a trainer role.

It took an unwillingness to be deterred and a willingness to fail to get my first training role in my organisation.

I surprised myself when I said, "I want to be a trainer, so either facilitate a training opportunity for me, at least part-time, or I'll quit."

Thankfully, I was recognised as an asset to the company so when I handed in my notice without another job to go to, it was rejected. Yep, my department Director rejected my resignation letter.

I wouldn't take it back but agreed to think about it over the weekend and confirm my decision on Monday. So when I returned and confirmed my decision, it took a few days for something to be worked out.

Now, I'm not recommending that anyone else do this but it worked for me. What I do recommend, is letting quality work precede you and standing for what you truly want.

My training role started as a secondment but ended up becoming a permanent role and started me on a path to becoming a speaker. I would stay in that role for two years before I moved on to another training position.

It would be many, many years before I would be paid to speak. I first had to overcome the hurdle of seeing myself as a speaker, which then opened the door for me to get paid to speak.

Early on in my entrepreneurial journey, I came across a great young entrepreneur called Daniel Priestley, who talked about becoming a KPI.

Back then most people would have only thought this term relates to a key performance indicator. However, Dan was talking about becoming a Key Person of Influence.

One of the key messages he shared with us on the journey to becoming a KPI was that we were 'standing on a mountain of value'. We already knew and had experienced enough to give value to others.

I heard the message but it would take some years for me to act on this. I guess it's a bit like a seed that is planted, nothing much seems to be happening, but there is something going on, it just isn't visible. Given enough time it would become visible. I would get to that place where I realised my professional expertise as a trainer coupled with my personal experience was my mountain of value.

Have you recognised your own mountain of value?

It was this recognition that moved me from being an impressive Speaker to becoming a speaker that impresses.

Not impresses because I seek to look good, but impresses because I seek to connect and touch those I speak to and with, based on my truth.

When we connect and when we're touched, transformation happens.

I started The Like Me CIC in 2018 and I started with speaking. I ended unemployment by starting my own business. Becoming unemployed and going on benefits for the first time in my life, whilst pregnant for the first time after being made redundant for the first time, was really tough. The Like Me CIC was named this because it was for women and girls like me.

This was my third attempt at entrepreneurship and what had felt like a curse was actually a blessing.

Being unemployed and on benefits entitled me to business development support, something I had never undertaken in my previous business attempts. I had never done more than an A4 business plan, (maybe that's why my businesses hadn't worked out!).

The guidance and mentoring to create my business meant I started with a detailed business plan and cash flow forecast, things I hadn't previously done. It made all the difference.

This organisation I had worked with also held networking events and invited me to share about The Like Me CIC and what we planned to do.

I received such a positive response to my speaker presentation, with people interested in partnering before I had even started. It was encouraging. It reminded me that I was an impressive Speaker but speaking my truth and sharing my expertise combined with my experience was a little way off. Nevertheless, the breeding ground for recognising the mountain I was standing on had begun.

I attended an inspirational event called The Women Like Me Luton Conference in 2018 which was well attended and thoroughly inspiring with a range of diverse women coming together and sharing their stories without shame or judgement. At the end of the event, there was a call to action which asked who would put this event on next year as Luton Council didn't want to do it again.

I wanted to put both hands and feet in the air and shout 'ME!'. However, I left with a determination that I'd be the one organising that conference the following year… and I did.

The Women Like Me Luton Conference was for women who had endured trauma but who refused to allow those hardships to define them. I also started The Girls Like Me Luton Conference for girls who may be enduring abuse or bullying, yet trying to function. Both conferences were about creating a safe space for us to share our stories of pain and triumph so as to encourage and empower one another. It was here that I began to share from my mountain.

Up until this point, I had been speaking whenever the opportunity arose. I spoke to people's minds. However, I still hadn't seen or pitched myself as a speaker so I wasn't actively seeking opportunities to speak. And to be honest, at my first conference, I hadn't properly planned what I was going to say. Nevertheless, I hosted and spoke and I began to see the value in my mountain.

I didn't share too much of my story because I was scared to be vulnerable.

But sharing what I did, and allowing others to share too, meant I saw that there was power in sharing your story, in sharing your truth. There was power in that daring V, as I call it, vulnerability.

Although, I still had some way to go on my journey as a speaker, I had started. I was beginning to realise that I was a Speaker, and I had something of value to share.

Have you shared from your mountain of value?

If not, what are you waiting for?

Even without much planning and preparation of what I was going to say, what I shared seemed to impress the ladies in that room. I spoke to their hearts as well as their minds, something I had never done before.

If you have shared from your mountain, well done! Keep going and keep growing. As at this stage of my speaker journey I was only sharing from my personal experience. I was half way there.

Life was about to hit rock bottom. The realisations I was undergoing as a speaker were nothing compared to the realisations I was having in the rest of my life.

My relationship was toxic and abusive, I wanted out. I wasn't being physically abused, but I felt like I was reliving my childhood. I'll share an indication of how bad that was shortly.

Entering into unimaginable depths, such as a refuge, rocked my world to the core. Yet it freed me. I lost my fear of shame and embraced vulnerability. It was after this that I began to share freely, with an openness I never had before. It was really scary but it was also really empowering for me and for those who heard. I stopped trying to appear so polished and put together. I stopped acting as if life was good when it wasn't. I became authentic.

It was soon after this that I came across the GTeX Community which offered business development and mentorship, something I desperately needed. I was doing the best I could in my business but I wasn't making the best use of my strengths.

Joining one of their programmes helped me to see where I was going wrong in not maximising my speaking abilities. I worked flat out on my business and to get my life moving forward.

Being busy and being effective aren't necessarily the same.

In my case they certainly weren't. I was putting on events and virtual training but wasn't getting anywhere close to hitting the numbers I wanted, literally or financially. My business was still a hobby, based on income generation.

Joining the GTeX Community was a turning point.

I realised my business growth depended on me acknowledging and using the gift I've always had, the ability to speak.

I was, and still am, an impressive Speaker, who through overcoming the obstacles I have faced in life, and embracing the lessons in them, have been able to realise that I am not defined by what I have been through.

Being vulnerable and sharing what I have been through doesn't diminish my value, it speaks of my endurance and resilience, allowing me to connect deeply with others.

I have balanced out my approach as Speaker and Trainer to use what I term the 'double P approach'.

I don't just share about my personal experiences to inspire, I also couple this with my professional expertise as a trainer.

I understand how people learn and have learned some great methodologies which I share to empower and enable development and growth of employees and entrepreneurs so they can unleash their potential and achieve.

The combination is powerful, I'd even go as far as to say it's transformational. Life changes when we do, and things change when our thinking changes. Our thoughts precede our feelings and actions. Once I saw myself as the Speaker that I had always been, I began to make waves as they say.

I didn't realise how fear of exposure had limited me to only speaking at my events and seeing as event management really isn't my thing, they often weren't as well attended as I wanted. Therefore, my platform was reduced.

By shifting my thinking to looking for speaking opportunities with those who already had the platform, I was advancing myself and my business.

By speaking, both to inspire and empower, I was building my brand. Refusing to be overly concerned about people paying me and seeking to maximise speaking platforms and the opportunities they offer, I got myself out there and began to build my credibility.

I knew I was a good Speaker, now I wanted to show the world that I was a speaker who impressed. I touched hearts and minds. I gave tools and techniques from that Speaker platform which made a difference.

And, if I was booked for leadership development and wellbeing training, I could empower individuals to make their own transformation in spite of what they may have been through.

We all have dreams and one of mine was to do a TED/TEDx talk. I knew very little about them but knew enough to know that it was a major achievement, something which seemed to cement your credibility as a speaker. I wanted to do one of those one day.

That day came a lot sooner than I expected.

Being part of the GTeX Community I was offered the opportunity to prepare for a TEDx talk and I thought why not, I am building my profile as a speaker after all.

I soon learned the difference between TED and TEDx and how close I was to a TEDx.

There was one in Bedford and they were holding an event in a few months.

I was determined to be on that line up, so I 'stalked' TEDx Bedford and finally someone got in touch. I was sent a form to complete and submit to see if I could be a part of the line-up. I was told if I didn't make it that year, I'd be put forward for the next year. However, they didn't understand that I am a woman of faith and how determined I am. I was GOING to be on that year's line-up.

My faith and determination paid off, I made it!

I took this opportunity to share with the greatest vulnerability, so much so it really troubled me. The night before my talk I couldn't sleep.

You see when I share about what I have been through, it's never to vilify those who have hurt me, it's simply me speaking my truth and sharing my story of what I have endured and managed to overcome.

What we've been through, good and bad, makes us who we are. When we share our truth we remove the shame and reclaim our power.

I felt the fear and did it anyway. I delivered a powerful TEDx Talk titled 'Stop Hiding; Show Up & Shine'. Feel free to check it out and leave a comment, I'll reply.

I was a Speaker and I owned it. Shortly after this, I was nominated for and won two Speaker awards! How amazing.

What we believe, we receive and I believed in myself as a Speaker as well as a Trainer.

Within a year of doing my TEDx talk I had made some strides, speaking on the Keynote stage at the PA Show was one of them. Unfortunately, the footage was lost for that. I also secured my first paid speaking gig at an International Women's conference. My speaker status was solidified.

My speaker journey, like my life, has been...interesting. It's allowed me to go beyond. Beyond what merely looks great or impressive, to what feels as great as it looks. Sharing from my mountain of value has empowered me to go beyond impressive to authentic and impressed.

CHAPTER 6

Be Prepared

By Kevin Harvey

Public speaking is a skill that many people find daunting, intimidating, and frightening, but it is also one of the most valuable skills to possess in today's world. Throughout my life, I have had the opportunity and privilege to hone my public speaking skills through various speaking experiences. In this chapter, I'll share my journey and offer practical tips and insights I've learned. Join me as we explore the rewarding art of Speaking in Public.

For as long as I can remember, I've always put my hand in the air, volunteering to speak in public. School plays, reading out loud in class, you name it, I was up for it, even if it meant wearing the obligatory tea towel on my head in the Christmas nativity.

My first taste of experiencing a large audience came when I was 8. I was in the Cubs, the boy scouts' junior section.

I was asked if I would like to take part in a large gathering that was taking place at Nottingham University on behalf of the scouts in front of many local dignitaries and high-ranking officials.

I would be given a small speech to present lasting about three minutes that I would have to learn and deliver.

The address was sports related and about the importance of focusing on the task. I sat with my father, learning the words for hours until I'd nailed it. That's when he said to me. "Now you have to perform it".

Before I was born my father had "Tread the boards" in local clubs and music halls, where he had met my mother, who was playing in an accordion band; The stage was in my blood.

He taught me how important it was to pause…. And use my body's actions to get the point over.

I felt nervous as I approached the microphone.

Nobody told me there would be a microphone.

For a split second, my mind went blank, my palms became sweaty, and I could feel my heart racing.

I took a deep breath, and then, as I slowly exhaled, my preparation took over, and off I went.

I looked past the audience and forgot that the microphone was there.

All I remember was saying the last line.

"Remember, always keep your eye on the ball." And as I said that last line, I lifted my hand, pointed to my eye, and then made a ball shape with both hands. Paused. And said thank you.

My audience stood up! Clapped loudly in appreciation. I was hooked.

I learnt many lessons from that short presentation that would serve me later in life. The use of nonverbal communication, how to pause when speaking, overcoming nerves, not being phased when faced with something unexpected like a microphone, and most importantly, something I teach today as a speaking coach and trainer—the Cub Scouts' motto written by its founder Robert Baden-Powell in 1908. "You are always in a state of readiness in mind and body to do your duty". "Be Prepared".

Next up was an even bigger venue, the Theatre Royal in Nottingham, where I was about to experience my first non-verbal experience and impromptu performance.

It was now 1971, and I was nine years of age. The show that night was "The Black and White Minstrel Show". They would be controversial today, but in the '70s, they were top billing. Appearing with them was a well-known local ventriloquist named Neville King. He was often on TV performing on the "Good Old Days "and later the "Generation Game" with his vent dummy "The Old Man".

My Dad knew him from his club days, and I was delighted to be sat on the 2nd row of the stalls. Part of Neville's act was to pick a youngster out of the audience, sit them on his knee and perform using the child as his Dummy. He recognised my Dad sitting in the second row, and you guessed it. I was chosen.

It was a non-speaking role apart from the "What's your name" and "Where are you from" as an introduction.

You probably won't remember an artist called Al Jolson, who dressed and wore make-up like the Minstrels, he was the most prominent artist in the world in the 1920s and the first guy to speak in the movies. That film was "The Jazz Singer."

So, I was, sitting on a ventriloquist's knee and miming while he threw his voice towards me and sang Jolsons classic "Climb upon my knee Sonny Boy" with his mouth shut and manipulating me to the song. You wouldn't get away with that today!

Jolson was one of my Dad's favourite artists and one of our house's most endlessly played LPs. I knew every word. As he reached the climax of his performance, this 9-year-old stood up, adopted the famous Jolson stance of dropping down to one knee with his arms outstretched, and I sang the closing lines from the song. Much to the amazement of Neville and the capacity audience of 1,247. (I looked it up).

It may have been serendipity that it happened, who knows, but one thing was sure, I was prepared in an extraordinary way. I had improvised and used nonverbal body language again; however, my most significant insight was climbing the stairs to the main stage from the stalls and looking out at the first few rows of people. I couldn't see any further back or up into the levels above due to the house lights being down and the bright spotlights shining on me. I was in my element.

I remember this moment every time I walk on stage.

Don't worry about the audience looking at you. Enjoy the moment and, in the words of Jolson in the first ever talkie. "You ain't heard nothing yet."

I followed this up with numerous school plays, and my confidence grew with the more things I got involved in.

The next notable memory was when at about 14, my school asked for candidates to apply for a position on the school council for my year. I had been active in a few school productions but was now a teenager with other things on my mind. The other pupils would choose the representative after performing a speech in the assembly the following week. I applied and was given a slot along with four other hopefuls. I made the fatal mistake of leaving my preparation to the last minute. I was ready to pull out the day before as I hadn't written anything, never mind practising it. Fortunately, you were allowed to read it, but I still couldn't be bothered, and then I found out that one of the girls I fancied in form 4P had applied and was the favourite to win the race for the girl representative.

I saw the opportunity to win two prizes.

But what was I going to speak about?

Elvis. I had been listening to his double album "40 Greatest Hits", and everybody I knew at school had a copy and was Elvis mad.

Whilst pondering on my topic, I looked at the album cover notes.

It was one minute short of the required time, so I wrote a 30-second opening as to why I would talk about Elvis and a 30-second big finish about his music's impact and how he inspired people.

Just for the record, I collected both prizes. Although my preparation had initially been poor, the thought of the reward, talking about something I was passionate about, and previous preparation work had given me the edge. Thinking outside the box, I'd presented something topical and inspirational to my audience. Again this would prove to be a significant insight later in my life when performing. One of the critical points in your preparation is "Knowing Your Audience".

My speaking took a back seat during my exams as I focused on my core subjects of music and drama. Music had taken over my life. I spent hours and hours practising at home to improve my playing skills.

As a trombone player, the neighbours were never happy, but that didn't stop me. I loved the thrill of being on a stage, whether playing in Brass bands, Jazz Orchestras, Classical Orchestras or in the pit at Operas and Musicals.

The practice and preparation were again paying off for me. But deep down, I knew I would never be centre stage doing this, only a band member.

That was fine as It opened up a fantastic world for me and gave me the privilege of playing at some of the top venues in the UK and Europe, including, The Concertgebouw in Amsterdam, the Beethoven Hall in Stuggart and conducted by Sir Andrew Lloyd Webber at The Royal Albert Hall.

The question was, should it be my career? Should I apply to University or a Music Academy? I was still determining my future. My music teacher from school came to the house to persuade my parents that I should go.

Whilst I had studied hard and practised hard at my music studies, I had done nothing for the other A levels and was worried that I would let my parents down if I failed them, as I would have to do another year of study. Three months before I was due to take my A levels, I quit education and started work. This wasn't the first job interview I'd gone for.

At my first interview, I got off the bus too early and had to walk for half a mile. My new suit was drenched when I arrived at the building with seconds to spare. I'd forgotten my coat. My heart was racing, and my palms were sweaty. This was unnatural for me, and I felt incompetent and uncomfortable.

The first question was, "What's the one thing that lets you down?" "That's easy; others can easily distract me." He thanked me for coming and said he'd be in touch!

As I left the building, it was evident that I wouldn't get the job, and I received the thank you but no thanks letter later. I hadn't planned my journey, made a terrible 1st impression, and hadn't realised I might be asked questions!

I was now working as a dispatch clerk in a warehouse, and whilst there were better places to improve my speaking skills, it was an excellent grounding in working with people from all walks of life.

I was still getting jobs as a gigging musician in the evenings and keeping my hand in performing.

I was asked to be the best man at a work colleague's wedding. I took to the task and spent hours preparing my speech.

I was full of confidence until 20 mins before I was about to speak when the bride's mother asked if she could see my speech. I showed her, and she told me what I could say and couldn't. I had not prepared for this; over half of my script was condemned. I quickly scribbled down some notes and made adjustments. I remember saying, "What a lovely special couple", about four times as I stumbled through. It had been a disaster from my point of view; however, years later, I reminded myself of this story when I help people write and perform their wedding speeches. So many of them come to me with preconceived ideas about what they should say. I tell them this story to help them prepare for all eventualities.

It wasn't long before I was noticed within the company and asked if I would like to help set up a new company they had purchased for six weeks in Leeds, 80 miles away. I jumped at the opportunity.

After six weeks, if willing to relocate, I was offered a management position. I was 23 years of age. My life changed. My speaking career was limited to sacking and interviewing people during this time. Within the first week, I had to employ eight new staff, and I interviewed 25 people. This was unlike anything I had ever done before. Talk about learning on the job.

The night before, the first time I sacked somebody, I wrote down what I would say and worked out how I would say it. Whilst an unpleasant task, the guy was relatively calm about it and understood the reasons. I didn't need to use the hammer hidden under my desk—a different type of preparation.

My career took off, and a few years later, I was made a company director and was involved In running staff training programmes and entertaining our clients at sportsman dinners, corporate events, and team-building days. I took all of this in my stride. I advanced my career by reading about Self Development and attending local events with some great speakers, and I decided that one day it would be me.

I was invited onto the Committee for the Yorkshire Trade Association and became dinner secretary organising the annual dinner and booking the speakers. I loved it, and a few years later, I was invited to be the Chairman. My job was to introduce the top table of trade experts and professional speakers. This needed some serious prep work. I went out on a limb. I introduced each one with jokes about them, most of which are unrepeatable today.

My after-dinner and stand-up routine was born.

I was now being asked to other trade events as the guest speaker, and whilst I spoke about the trade, it was the comedy and humour that the audience loved. I talked at rugby clubs, local societies, book launches and prestigious events like the NSPCC annual dinner in front of 400 people. I developed my skills as an MC and Auctioneer; My preferred payment was out-of-pocket expenses and fees donated to charity.

I spent ten years running my event, "Legends in your Local", hiring pubs and clubs to provide an affordable opportunity for people to meet their sporting legends rather than expensive black-tie events. I hosted the events with my comic introductions, now a 30-minute stand-up routine. I always dressed as a different character and adjusted my act to suit the celebrity speaker.

I was loving life and doing what I loved. Then it all came crashing down.

I did nothing for 18 months except become a victim. I was out of work, divorced, living in a rental and drinking too much.

Eventually, I decided to do something about it and reread all of the self-development books I had bought over the years, which had become shelf-development books gathering dust.

I enrolled in a 12-week Speaking in Public Course and upgraded my previous coaching qualifications.

I used these skills to sort myself out and came through this period with a positive mindset. I had studied body language, I was an NLP Master practitioner and a qualified hypnotherapist, and most importantly, I had experience working with an audience and writing material. I knew where I was heading next.

I prepared for my first Motivation speech. The subject content was something that nobody knew more about. ME. This was the hardest thing I'd written. I named the talk "Breakdowns to Breakthroughs" and was about to bare my soul to an audience.

What will people think of me when I tell them I was a failure? Will they think I'm bragging when I tell them how I turned my life around and that it's always possible to make changes no matter where or how old you are?

I had invited 10 of my close friends and hadn't told them what I was speaking about. They also weren't aware of the full extent of my depression, as I always tried to be the life and soul of a party when I was out with them.

They all arrived early and decided to sit in the front row, and as I recalled the previous few years of my life, I remember looking directly at them as I talked about the importance of having a sound support system around me. I was an emotional wreck, and I felt my emotions taking over, but experience kicked in, and I looked past them and regained my composure.

Writing and performing this speech was one of the most therapeutic things I've ever done, and I recommend that everybody puts this on their bucket list.

The evening went well, and I couldn't wait to see the video that had been taken of the event. Although the event had given me more bookings to speak in London and several other big cities, the video proved that I wasn't as well prepared as I thought and still had plenty to learn.

The microphone didn't clip onto my shirt correctly, and all you could hear as I walked onto the stage was the clinking sound of my wooden-soled shoes. But the biggest issue was how much I was still in victim mode. I had seen many speakers go through the same thing when performing, but the great speakers would mention specific facts but hadn't dwelled on them.

A motivational speech aims to inspire and motivate the audience, not to make the speaker the centre of attention or to provoke pity from the listeners. The focus should be on hope, inspiration, and practical steps for achieving success.

I still love speaking today, but as I get older, I have found so much more satisfaction in training and coaching people, giving them the confidence to speak in public, whether it's to help with relationships, wedding speeches, Interview techniques or presenting at work or promoting themselves for business.

Preparation is about more than just the content. It's about dealing with everything technical, expressing yourself, showing emotion, and understanding what the audience wants and expects.

Public speaking doesn't have to be scary or intimidating.

Just remember the first lesson I learnt from my first speech aged 8.

"You are always in a state of readiness in mind and body to do your duty". "Be Prepared".

CHAPTER 7

From Shy Girl to Public Speaker

By Lisa M. Billingham

My entrance into public speaking was decidedly unglamorous. I lacked the confidence to speak to anyone in everyday conversation, so standing in front of an audience to do it was a massive no-no; in fact, public speaking had never entered my head; it wasn't a lifelong goal, and, it was the furthest thing from my mind so I suppose you could say, it started by accident.

I worked (slogged my guts out for next to nothing) in the corporate world for over two decades. Instead of leaving the job, which I didn't like much, I went for a promotion (enter people pleaser imposter.) I only intended to stay there until the end of my three-month probationary period and had been searching for jobs, attending interviews, and filing rejections for any and every role I could lay my hands on for the entire time I was there. Then, one day, I was offered the job in the first interview. My head was screaming say yes, take it. Out of my mouth came, "I'll think about it and let you know." Yes, I turned down that job.

Being given false hope, where I was, that things would change when, in truth, it was me that needed to change. I had to stop doing things to please others and find the confidence to make my own decisions. I often wonder what life would have been like had I said yes at that interview. Too late now, though; I'd taken the promotion.

This pushed me outside my comfort zone, and I retrained for my new role.

It did me a favour and helped me build my confidence, although I didn't see it at the time.

The promotion forced me into public speaking, albeit in a small and informal way. I had to do sales presentations to prospective clients, some went down well, and I won the business, some not so well and … well, I didn't. Did I enjoy it? No. Was I good at it? Probably not, but no one ever told me either way.

I was still not right after my breakdown; why had I taken a promotion? I should probably explain here a little about my breakdown. Working two and a half jobs. Yes, I had a full-time, full-on job, plus I was doing project work and a casual job in the evening too. I was in and out of bad relationships, and I was broken. I'd hit the proverbial brick wall. I couldn't function properly. One Tuesday afternoon, I left the office knowing I wouldn't be at work for a while. I was finally going to the doctor. Armed with a diagnosis of stress, anxiety and depression, a prescription for Sertraline and a promise of an appointment with a mental health nurse and the words "do something nice, don't sit around at home." I left the surgery. What was 'nice', though. I didn't enjoy anything I was doing, except my part-time job, and I couldn't do that having a sick note; what now? I wandered around town, and a poster in a shop window caught my eye.

Relaxation classes there, starting the following evening. A five-week course. I could do that. Couldn't I? Standing staring at the poster. Stuck to the ground, not having the confidence to even enquire about the sessions, but it was my lucky day.

The owner of the business was coming out, and she started chatting with me about it. After showing me around the centre, she booked me in. I still had to get myself to these damn classes though. Would I be able to do it? Would everyone be looking at me and laughing? I knew I had to go to these classes. I knew the layout after my tour, so that helped, but shaking like a leaf, I put the upset stomachs aside and with a banging heartbeat, I attended the first class. I lay on the floor at the start of the first session after the introductions and realised all of the ladies there were broken, just like me.

The next chapter in my life had begun, and we were in this together. Lots more courses and training followed, then life-changing surgery followed by redundancy. Again, I asked myself that question. What now?

While recovering from the surgery and suspecting I would be made redundant, I read self-help and business books and decided to become self-employed. I set up a business using my coaching, therapy and mediumship skills to help others find their confidence and live a life they love. Laughable at the time as I was still struggling, but, it's true what they say, while you're teaching, you're also learning.

Many of the self-employment experts/gurus, whatever you call them, told me I needed to write a book and become a speaker. "Eh," and "why" were my well-thought-out and formulated responses. "To get your message out there," was the reply. Great, I thought, let's do it. So, I spent thousands of pounds and just as many hours with coaches and consultants trying to figure out how to 'perfect' my speaking voice and my message and deliver it to an audience. Did I enjoy it? No. Did it work? Erm... No. Did I carry on, regardless? Yes.

I had my first break or speaking event at a networking meeting. A friend offered 10-minute slots to new business owners and those new to public speaking. To say I was nervous was an understatement. I was ****ing myself. I fluffed my lines, I finished short of my time, my throat felt like it was closing up, and I had to keep taking deep breaths. I tried to do everything I had been 'taught' to do, but whilst it was well received, it didn't set the world on fire as I hoped it would. I still had much to learn, not from others but from myself. At this point, I was becoming increasingly exhausted and haemorrhaging money like it grew on trees. (It doesn't, by the way.) I had to decide, so I chucked in the towel, closed the business and went to work abroad.

At this point, it's fair to say that until very recently, I hadn't been on an aeroplane for over a decade (to Jersey), and I hadn't been abroad for 19 years.

Didn't like flying. My experience on the flight to Jersey, where every movement felt like an off-road expedition, but in the air, had put me off flying. I was never doing it again… Or so I thought.

My confidence had taken many kicking's over the years, I didn't know who I was, and in truth, by going to work abroad, I was running away. I didn't know that at the time, but I was. I got on the plane, travelled to Menorca and guess what… Yep, part of my job meant I had to do public speaking. Was I ever going to get away from it?

At the tender age of 45, I was embarking on what I thought would be a new career as a holiday rep. In this role, I had to do the same thing again, sell services by standing in front of an audience. An audience which, in the main, didn't want to be there as most of them could do the 'speech' better than I could as they'd been travelling to the island for more years than I'd been on earth and knew it like the back of their hand. Have you ever tried selling ice to an Eskimo? No, me neither, but this is what I imagine it to be like, an uphill battle of wills. I learned a lot from these guests, some of which I used in my later welcome meetings.

Because I was abroad, in a different environment and well and truly outside my comfort zone, I found after a few weeks I enjoyed doing the welcome meetings and the airport bus speeches. I didn't, however, enjoy making a tit of myself, learning the dance routine for the group show we had to perform every week in the hotel I was based at. I should elaborate here. As I was working in an all-inclusive family hotel, there was so much going on, entertaining the children, including the big kids (adults,) and learning new systems and processes after being thrown in at the deep end. There's nothing quite like learning on the job, but it was hard work.

Additionally, the whole staff team had to perform a show once a week, so I was more stressed here than I had been at home. Feeling disillusioned, I requested a change of job or a flight home.

Luckily, I managed to do a job swap, but I compèred a show before I did. Rather than messing up the steps and risking everyone ending up in a heap on the stage because I was dancing on the wrong foot. (I dance now, but only for pleasure and not to perform.)

It didn't matter if I got the compèring wrong. Nobody, not even me, knew what would come out of my mouth.

To say that was by far the best experience and most fun I'd had to date was an understatement. The audience was engaged, even the children, the staff thought I was nuts (mmm, I'll let you decide on that point,) and I thoroughly enjoyed the evening.

Unfortunately, because I'd asked for a change of job, I wasn't allowed to compère any further shows, but it had served its purpose by then and at the back of my mind was and still is always a chance of that happening again.

Within a couple of weeks, I started my new job, travelling between hotels, delivering welcome meetings, and having fascinating conversations with new people.

Between stressful times and good times, I had to remind myself how far I'd come. Lacking confidence for the majority of my life, I was amazed I was there at all.

Looking in the mirror, I didn't recognise the person looking back at me. As I continued through that season, my confidence grew, I discovered a love of skinny dipping, and I became good at public speaking and delivering welcome meetings and bus speeches.

After the first few weeks, I abandoned the scripts I was given (please don't tell my old boss) and began speaking from the heart, including my personal experiences, whether good, bad or indifferent. I was telling it how it was. Or at least how it was for me. In doing this, I would get the audience's empathy or excitement and sometimes tell them how awful my experience was, enticing them to buy so they could prove me wrong. I was being honest. I couldn't say whether one trip was better for them than another. Or could I? I seemed to have an uncanny way of knowing what would suit people. Because I'd closed the business, I didn't feel like I was using those skills in this job, but I was, all of them.

Speaking at these welcome meetings and on airport transfer buses started me thinking about all the skills I have. All the knowledge I've gained through my life experiences and, let's face it making mistakes.

How could I get these messages out there? Sharing the experiences of an exceptionally good trip with my guests and listening to their glowing feedback was one thing. And it was great. But something was missing. After a season and a half of working abroad, I was brought back down to earth with a bang and the onset of covid. Landing in Birmingham at the end of March 2020, I asked the question again. What now? No more welcome meetings and bus chats; instead, a temporary, (at least I hoped it was) situation where I found myself staring at four walls in a makeshift office (spare bedroom,) wondering what to do. It didn't take me long to decide. I was going to write my book.

Another new skill I was learning. I'd discussed this with coaches previously, and now I had the time to do it. I knuckled down and wrote what became a self-help novel based on my life experiences, not the business book all these coaches had told me I should write. Because the book touches on some tough controversial subjects such as mental health, domestic abuse and life-changing surgery, it has changed the lives of many of its readers.

But I digress. When I began writing the book, I also started networking again. Albeit online due to the world situation. I was talking about my experiences and how I'd come to write the book, and I discovered many of the people I was meeting had been through, were going through or knew someone in the same situations as I had been in. It resonated with them; this was amazing and gave me the courage to finish and publish the book.

After publication, that age-old question raised its head for me again. What now? The coaches who told me I needed to write a business book (oops, I went a little wrong there) also told me I needed to speak about my experiences. The cogs in my brain started to work overtime again and purely by chance. (Or was it?) The world began to re-open, and I could attend events or run my own.

Throughout this journey or adventure, as I call it, I grew spiritually, mentally and emotionally. I half expected lockdown to tip me over the edge again, but all the work I'd done on my mental health following my breakdown had helped me deal with the situation differently, and I started honing another of my skills, which I'd all but forgotten about. My ability to connect to the spirit world to deliver messages to those left behind. What is she talking about, I hear you cry.

After my breakdown, I tried every imaginable therapy, counselling, coaching service, and relaxation technique known to humankind. Still, I couldn't get out of the fog clouding my brain. After much nagging, my friend persuaded me to go and see a medium, and to keep her quiet; I did. This was yet another catalyst for change, and I was amazed at the information she gave me. Subsequently, I went to many mediums over the next few years. I found comfort and solace in knowing my loved ones still looked out for me, but I needed more. I had to find a way forward in my life and wanted to understand mediumship. I did many years' worth of research, and while scrolling through social media feeds, I came across an advert with the headline, "Are you psychic?" Was it pure chance I'd seen this, or was this divine intervention at play? I didn't even question it, as the medium had said to me that I should sit in a circle. At the time, I had no idea what she meant, but I understood once I responded to the advert and attended the classes on offer. It was a safe place to hone my skills and gain the support of others doing the same. The lady taking the class made me give evidence first. (Enter nerves again) you can see a pattern here, can't you? I did as she asked, and although there was only a little information, it was my first time. Most of the information I gave the recipient could take. I continued researching, taking various courses and workshops and sitting in the circle for many years. Continually learning and growing and helping others to do the same.

As the world continued to open up, I began speaking at networking events, schools and my events. Subjects ranged from confidence and mental health to spirituality and healing through creative writing. All of these have an element of intuition and spirit, and all are delivered from my heart to yours. Each platform is a playground. Every speech, event, Q&A or mediumship event is different. Every audience member will take away something different, and I also learn and grow at these events. By speaking from the heart, I know the messages will get through wherever they are needed. I never imagined I would speak on stage. I was too shy, and nervous and my confidence was always zero or close to it.

I love it and aim to speak at the O2 in London to a full house, c20,000 people. Then who knows where after that? If I can do it, so can you.

Grab life with both hands and live your dreams. Don't let anyone or anything stand in your way.

CHAPTER 8

The Accidental Speaker

By Martin Sharp

Some people are born great. Some have greatness thrust upon them. And others open their mouths and have to rise to the challenge.

The question is, which one are you?

Come to think of it, which one am I?

Let me take you back to a cold, wet grey morning in early January 2014, and you find me sitting in another corporate meeting room in Uxbridge, just outside London in the UK. You know, the type of meeting room with a horseshoe style layout of light oak wooden desks for up to 10 people, though you can always squeeze 12 in like today easily.

Those uncomfortable grey padded chairs without casters and with everyone facing the large black LCD screen at the opening, slowly being tortured with death by PowerPoint by the world's most boring grey haired, balding and overweight man, Wild Bill.

His ill-fitting double-breasted dark grey suit on his marathon tour to cure chronic insomniacs, he drones on in a monotone nasally American voice adding barely more value than reading the slides on information that could have easily been read in 10 minutes and didn't need a 90-minute meeting to convey.

However, he clearly likes the sound of his own voice. The airless room is filled with the pungent smell of office workers, stale coffee and recirculated air. The blank, vacant, zombie-like looks on all those who are in attendance, everyone trying to avoid eye contact and no one daring to yawn.

Though visibly relieved as the presentation draws to its conclusion, which could be paraphrased as "well, we don't know what to do or where to start", only put in more flowery corporate language.

"We need to agree on the approach to ascertain what is included and the method we will employ to move this across. Without agreement on these fundamental basics, this initiative will be unsuccessful again in defining the $16 billion digital assets and how they will be transitioned safely," I explain.

All eyes wheel around to look at me with a mixture of hope and fear on their faces, like a hungry lion that has been let into the gazelle enclosure, only they know they won't be eaten today.

"Well", Wild Bill retorts sarcastically, with a sly grin growing across his face, "you should do that then! You are obviously the most experienced here, having delivered over 12 successful transitions in other mergers and acquisitions, and we've failed to achieve anything like this over the last nine months! I'll tell you what, I'll give you until the end of March to gain agreement and present a clear plan."

So the stage was set. We gathered some fantastic change agents I'd worked with over the years on previous transitions. Project managers, enterprise architects, data and systems specialists, analysts, trainers and communications experts set to work speaking to many people from across both companies and trawling through so many documents that would probably rival the archives at the British Library to answer the fundamental questions.

Within the next few weeks, the essence of a plan at a high level was broadly agreed upon by everyone on what they were exchanging.

However, no one knew where these were stored or how to disentangle them from the remainder of the business. And the arguments and disagreements that this generated were like a polarising subject being debated in the Houses of Parliament, with people within their own companies not even able to agree on the simplest things. Some were being stubborn for the sake of it and argued the equivalent of the sky is green, and the grass is blue. The "yes" men were trying to gain favour with their boss, while others were withholding information based on knowledge is power, and they didn't want to be out of a job, not that the idea was ever mentioned.

Despite the behaviour of some, by the end of February, we had a rough outline of what was included and a broad plan of how it could transition. Everyone in the European offices from both companies were behind the plan, though the Americans were still not entertaining it. We arranged a three-week road trip to visit each of the major centres in the US to see if an in-person meeting would help.

About this time, I'd finished reading another business book that a friend recommended, as he knew I had set a target to read 1000 business books in my life.

The content was interesting about presenting, and I was happy to accept all the help I could with the upcoming presentations I needed to give.

So I picked up my mobile and dialled the number for the office.

"Hi, I'm Martin Sharp, I've just read Passion into Profit, and it says to contact you to discuss the next steps on how you can help me with presentation skills," I ask. "Ah yeah, mate, you need to come to the Public Speakers University; it's a four-day event, and we have one coming up in May. Will it just be you, or are you bringing a friend or colleague?" in what sounds like a Cockney wide boy voice to my Yorkshire man's ear. I laugh loudly, though unfairly. "I'm sorry, I'm just at the start of a work engagement that is going to keep me very busy for the next 18-24 months, and I could do with something to help with some presentations next week. Do you have anything else available?" there is an audible pause on the phone like I could almost hear the cogs whirring. "Well, we have the World No1 Expert Training online course that you can do; it is £197 and goes through some more detail about how to be seen as an expert through delivering a great presentation?" the Londoner replies.

"Ok, I'll go with that!". I pay with my credit card, and Craig invites me to get back in touch when I get time to join them on the course.

Downloading the 12 hours of course content to my laptop, I watch it in double time during the 8-hour flight between Manchester and JFK airports. Learning about how to improve presentation skills, create an engaging opening to a presentation, and improve the likelihood of agreement during your presentation. My mind is whirring as I consider how I could apply some of these concepts.

I am barely aware of the transit through the airport, collecting my bags and travelling to our first meeting in New York. As the black Chrysler Suburban Taxi pulls up outside the huge skyscraper, I finish briefing my team on the plan.

We are ushered through to a grand-looking long boardroom. The dark mahogany wood oval table has been polished to a mirror finish. Place settings laid out, each with a hand-stitched tan leather desk pad, with a recess for the water-filled crystal glass tumbler and another for the black Parker pen trimmed in silver with the company logo on. There must be over 60 people crammed into the room, with what is clearly a pecking order of the key stakeholders taking their place at the table.

The second row of chairs had been placed behind the first, with those sitting precariously balancing their laptops and notepads on their knees and around the edge, standing includes everyone else.

We have reserved space near the projector screen and flipcharts at the end of the table. Wild Bill is already seated with his hands behind his head, elbows sticking out at each side, leaning back in his chair with a smug grin.

I look around the room at everyone in a variety of business dress, many of the faces I recognised from the video conference calls, though seeing them in person reminded me of the meeting at the start of the year, with the same mixture of hope and fear on their faces.

My palms start sweating as I hastily set up my laptop, and my team takes their seats. I can't hear anything in the room, for the pounding of the blood rushing through my ears. I turn to face the flip chart, more to find a moment to take a breath, control the urge to run away and compose myself than any real need to write the name of the project on the page. After all, everyone knew why we were there. That said, I'd never held a room with this number of people before, and this was the biggest transition I'd ever architected.

I turn around and address the whole room. "Would you agree that continuing to disagree is getting us nowhere?" there were a sea of nods, "and would you also agree that we have to do this, regardless of any personal reservations?" the nods were joined by quiet though audible grunts and yeses. I continued to lay out the problems and what the outcomes would be if they were addressed, along with subsequent consequences. Then moved into what good could look like, how both companies would benefit, and personal opportunities for advancements.

Following the presentation's opening structure, I learned during the flight and tried out some of the speaker archetypes and incidental phrases.

Three hours flew by, and we were only interrupted briefly by the appearance of the brown bag lunches. Discussion and debate continued over lunch; everyone engaged, finally reaching a consensus and starting to work on the details.

Wild Bill's grin has turned into a grimace; folding his arms tight against his body and slumping his shoulders forwards, he remains silent for the rest of the meeting. The planning continues late into the evening and only stops when it is time to travel to the next office.

The three weeks play out like groundhog day. We get a few hours of sleep, waking at 4 am to speak to the team in the UK to provide updates and direction. Then meet with the team in the US at 7 am for breakfast. By 9 am, we're at the company's office, where we repeat the presentation with a few amends due to the consensus raised.

The customary brown-bag working lunch arrives, though we press on and continue over dinner late in the evening before travelling to the next city. We travelled from New York to Raleigh, Philadelphia to Boston, Newark to New York to New Jersey and back around again. Each time reaching an agreement and gaining more momentum. The European offices had no objections to the proposed changes, so the work on making the transition a reality could begin.

Over the following 18 months, the plans were implemented, and the digital asset transfer was a success, passing all regulatory checks and exceeding the hopes of both organisations for the benefits they receive.

To this day, I don't know whether it was the preparation we'd done beforehand to lay the groundwork, the newly implemented presentation skills that I'd learnt on the first flight over or simply the fact that we'd "pressed the flesh".

The US teams looking at the whites of our eyes made the difference. Whatever it was, I knew I needed to develop my presentation skills further and master what I'd started to learn.

So true to my word, on the 11th of February 2016, I called Craig and booked to attend Public Speakers University starting on the 30th of June. There I learned six key skills needed to deliver informative presentations that drive change.

You need to be engaging from the start. People will judge you within seconds, and if they believe you are boring, not for them, or don't resonate with your message, it will be much harder to win them over later; you know that first impressions count, right?

Now, most speakers on stage, on screen or online, repeat what others do or want to get straight into the teaching and changing part, especially if they are trying to build consensus, strive for a person or business change or sell a product or service. Yet at this early stage in the presentation, you have four questions that are in the audience's mind that must be addressed first.

Without this, they may not agree with your message or relate it to themselves.

Next, you have to build a framework for your presentation so that you don't get lost and your audience has something to follow.

It's a bit like a map. When you give someone directions, with all the lefts, rights, straight-ons, etc., those listening may still not get to the destination, even if they are accurate.

By having a map, and a framework, your audience will always be able to know where you are and relate to this. Plus, if you go off-piste by answering a question or bringing up something you heard from one of the delegates earlier in the day or over lunch, you can bring yourself back on topic quickly and professionally.

Then it is time to learn some presentation skills so you don't come over as a monotone speaker hiding behind a lectern or podium.

Learning how to stand, walk, talk and the different archetypes so you can use them to captivate your audience rather than comatose them, along with how to create stories that help to move people emotionally and not just keep beating them over the heads with statements. Becoming a proficient storyteller is a skill that has enhanced humanity for thousands of years, used to pass on knowledge, warnings and news.

There are only a few story structures that work, and one that works well for illustrating the powerful effects of change, which is used even today in most blockbuster movies.

Creating content is always a worry, whether that is writer's block when authoring a book or staring at a blank PowerPoint slide when crafting a presentation. Yet questions create content, and learning how to use questions along with methods for challenging beliefs that will prevent change from occurring is a powerful tool in your armoury.

Finally, it comes down to inviting people to change, to take the next steps, and to make something happen. Because when it comes to presentations, just being sat there listening does not mean the outcomes will magically occur. It is the action that the audience takes afterwards that makes the difference.

As a presenter, have you served them enough for them to act, or did you serve them too much that they feel they no longer need anything else?

At first, I wasn't very good.

However, I knew these would be powerful skills to master, so I became a member of the Professional Speakers Academy.

Within the year, I became an award-winning international speaker, speaking across Europe, the Middle East, Central Asia and the US. Transforming businesses worldwide, changing the hearts and minds of so many to share their gifts, skills and knowledge, and being invited to become a speaking mentor and trainer for the Academy itself.

Now I use my newfound speaking skills to tackle the overweight and obesity crisis plaguing businesses and boardrooms worldwide, in what the World Health Organisation (W.H.O.) see as one of the fastest-growing demographics.

I should know; I was one of them, letting my business and helping others impact my health, growing to 154Kg that is 340lb with a 54" waist and all the corresponding aches, pains, lethargy and brain fog, to getting back to 94kg or 207lb with a 32" waist feeling fabulous, more confident and with a sharper mind.

Through developing the skill of speaking, it has allowed me to have a bigger impact on this important subject, for example in the first nine months of 2022 alone, I have been interviewed on nine podcasts, asked to share my message on TV and Radio 18 times and appeared on stage 12 times,

I've been able to use the same skills of positioning the audience, storytelling and creating transformational content for 46 magazines and press articles because I am seen as an expert in the field.

The ripple effect is so powerful, and every day someone sends me a message of thanks that they have hope and are making changes in their own lives.

You see, sometimes, when you open your mouth and share, the most wonderful things can happen that go far beyond what you may have imagined. So share your gifts with the world and be a powerful agent of change.

CHAPTER 9

A Shy Girl's Guide to Speaking

By Melitta Campbell

I remember the first time I spoke in public. I was ten years old, and it was not a great experience.

I had just moved from my home near London to my mother's hometown in Wales. My teacher loved that my accent was so different and insisted I open the school's Christmas carol concert. Being shy and still experiencing some culture shock, I was not keen. But my protests landed on deaf ears.

I barely slept leading up to the event. I neatly wrote out my words to help calm my nerves and glued them onto some festive golden card. Knowing I had my script to hand, I worried less about forgetting my words. But, on the day of the concert, as I stood up to speak, my teacher saw my card and, to my horror, took it away! "You don't need that, dear," she said with a smile.

I took my place at the front of the church. I looked out over the sea of strange faces and froze. I managed to mumble a few words but felt so self-conscious and dizzy that I ran back to my seat, warm tears quietly making tracks down my face. The feeling of shame and embarrassment followed me into my future, speaking for a long time. And I'm far from alone in this.

The fear of public speaking is very common. When I discuss it with others, they often refer to a childhood memory of stage fright or standing awkwardly at the front of the class. You may have your own version of this memory, which fills you with dread when you are called upon to speak.

In these moments, I've learned that it's important to challenge your memory and the negative thoughts that come with it. Do any of these sound familiar to you?

If I stand up and speak, people will laugh at me.

I'll only forget my words, and then people will think I'm incompetent.

I'm not important enough …pretty enough …interesting enough …funny enough (etc.)

Why would anyone listen to my story???

We've all had thoughts like these. It's our brain being helpful.

It's keeping us safe from any uncomfortable feelings that may follow if we speak up and things don't go perfectly.

However, I've also learned we don't have to listen to these thoughts. We can even challenge them! By doing this myself, I've managed to turn my inner critic into my inner cheerleader. This has enabled me to put many fears in their place and say 'Yes' to some exciting opportunities.

But I'm skipping ahead.

I didn't just wake up one day and start speaking on stage. It was quite a long journey. Let me take you back to me, age 29, when I worked in Geneva as the Head of Communications for a large International Private Bank.

Three things happened in close succession that prompted me to think that speaking in public might not be so terrifying after all.

#1. Our Chairman was opening a new company office in Dubai and needed a speech written for the event. Given my role, I was seen as the perfect person for the task.

While I'd written many articles, memos and reports for senior executives in my time, I'd never written a speech. I was excited at the prospect of exploring a different form of communication. However, I felt intimidated that my first speech was for such an auspicious occasion. With hindsight, this was the very criteria that pushed me to go 'all in'.

I closely analysed the world's best speeches, breaking down the patterns that made them so great. This was such a valuable exercise. I started to see the power of having a single clear purpose, using stories and metaphors, and how certain word patterns could amplify a feeling or message.

I also noticed they paid attention to how they wanted the audience to think and feel as the speech progressed. I knew I needed a single red thread that I could weave through each section of the talk. I needed to pay special attention to the key points and the manner in which I presented them. And I needed to take the audience on a journey to give them new perspectives and a deeper understanding of our mission and its relevance to their vision and goals.

I took time to craft a speech that considered these factors. It felt quite different from anything I'd previously produced, and I was happy with the result. Despite this, I remember just how nervous I was hitting 'send' and hearing the *swoosh* as my words sped over to the Chairman for review. I was even more nervous receiving his reply.

I stared at my inbox for a long time before opening the message.

One word. That's all he changed in the entire talk. Just one word! I was over the moon.

Since then, I've applied these lessons to all the speeches I have written, many of which have been spoken by leaders of Fortune 500 companies and UN agencies. These lessons have never let me down. They also taught me how the right structure could ease the job of the speaker, in turn helping keep nerves at bay.

#2. One of my colleagues invited me to attend a women's conference at the Bank's headquarters in London.

In my career, I'd never felt held back by being a woman, so I had never considered attending such an event. But my friend explained that it was a positive and uplifting experience, so I agreed to attend. I was so pleased that I did. Just as my friend had promised, it was an inspiring event. I loved every talk and every workshop. However, it was the keynote speaker who really captivated me. She didn't share just information–she shared a story! Her personal story. How she presented showed me how much we can captivate, encourage and inspire others by sharing our real-life experiences. They make our messages relatable and give them longevity. I can still remember her story to this day.

That experience prompted me to think differently about my presentations. I wanted to see if I could build stories around my key points to make them more inspiring and memorable.

I tested this idea in my team meetings first, with excellent results. I quickly noticed a shift in my ability to engage my team and keep their attention. The meetings became more enjoyable, too, as my stories created a stronger connection between everyone in the meeting.

Being someone who is introverted and prefers to think before they speak, taking some time to prepare one or two stories ahead of time proved a great tactic for me. Stories are also far easier for you to remember as a speaker too. It gave me the confidence to speak up more in meetings outside my department. As my confidence and ability to engage grew, so did my visibility and credibility, which led to the third event.

#3. I was promoted at work, meaning I would need to present regularly to colleagues across the Bank.

By now, I knew I could craft a good message. But I wanted to keep building my skills, particularly around my delivery, so I could captivate my audiences like the speaker I saw in

London. I'd seen how powerful stories could be in meetings, but I was also ready to step up and bring these more intentionally into my presentations.

That's when I discovered Toastmasters International, a public speaking club. Their bi-monthly meetings allowed me to further develop my public speaking skills and practice in a safe environment. I felt nervous before attending my first meeting. But once the meeting began and three people gave their prepared speeches, I knew I was in the right place. These speeches were interesting. They were creative. They were full of passion. And I loved all the ideas, lessons and stories the speakers shared. I quickly came to understand that there is no one special type of person who can give a great talk. You just need to be someone who wants to.

In the following months, I took in every word, every gesture and every piece of advice shared. From studying others and, over time, developing my delivery, I noticed a change in the way people responded to me in the office. When I gave presentations, people approached me at the end, asking for advice and I noticed that some of the fears I had previously felt, particularly around handling questions, had disappeared since I could now improvise and formulate my thoughts better.

My growing confidence and clarity had a positive impact on my team and their performance as well. It became clear to me that in the process of becoming a better communicator, I was becoming a better leader too. And this was having a knock-on effect elsewhere in my life.

I was also more self-assured while networking, for example. This led me to meet incredibly inspiring people who expanded my understanding of what is possible and introduced me to many opportunities. I was invited to speak and join prominent committees.

Thanks to my new skills and growing credibility, I was offered another promotion a few months later. One that saw me report directly to the company's CEO. I saw this as an opportunity to inspire more women to dream bigger for their careers. I proposed creating a forum where women could discuss their challenges, share ideas, feel safe, and be encouraged to speak up and network.

My new boss loved the idea, and I led this initiative over the next two years. It prompted a significant culture shift within the Bank. This reinforced for me that when you build your confidence and speak up, you become a leader who lifts others alongside them and creates positive change.

I'm so grateful for these three events. They taught me a lot about public speaking, such as the importance of a simple, clear structure and the power of sharing personal stories.

And most of all, they showed me that to become an impactful speaker, you don't need to have a particular personality or to look a certain way. You don't even need too much experience. You need to be someone who wants to speak up and share value.

So, if you are reading this, feeling that you could never stand up in front of an audience and speak. I'd like you to think again.

You don't have to present in front of thousands of people tomorrow. Just start somewhere.

To help you, here are the biggest lessons I learned early on in my journey:

1: Have a simple, straightforward structure for your talk that takes your audience on a journey of discovery. Avoid the temptation to overload your speech with information or to get too fancy and complicated. While the spoken word can be inspiring, it can only be said live once. The audience can't go back and reread a paragraph if they missed a point. So, keep it simple. Aim to have one clear purpose for your talk and use a maximum of three core messages to achieve this goal.

2: Share your stories and those of others. You may be tempted to think you have no interesting stories to share. But there is a lesson hidden in all our experiences. Challenge yourself to find these. Think of a random event that happened yesterday; what lesson could you extract from this? Our brains are hardwired to listen to stories and absorb the lessons they teach us. They engage and inspire us. And stories make your message enjoyable and memorable too.

3: Build your skills and confidence to speak up and lead. When you do, you will also elevate the people around you. Even if you don't have ambitions to speak on large global stages, everyone gains when you can share your ideas, lessons, passions and experiences with others. Break things down and take your time to grow into a great speaker and leader in a comfortable way. But do commit to getting started. I'm always amazed by how quickly our Toastmasters members grow in skills and confidence once they give their first talk. I'm excited to see what will happen for you too.

Looking back, I see how my speaking and stories have evolved along with my life experiences.

Along with tales of my corporate life, I can now add my reflections as a mother and an entrepreneur too.

My 'shy girl' theme has proven particularly popular. It has led me to be invited to speak around the world. So many people relate to the adventures and mishaps I've had since I started my journey to move from the shy girl I was to the speaker, coach and leader I'm continuing to grow into. It is an honour to share my stories and lessons, and I'm always humbled to hear how my experiences have helped someone else take an important step in their lives. After seeing the popularity of the theme, I turned my talk, 'A Shy Girl's Guide to Networking', into the first in a series of empowering books.

My growing reputation as a speaker, coach and mentor also allowed me to work with two TEDx events in Switzerland and the UK. Being part of a network of speaker coaches focused on helping people with 'ideas worth spreading' take to the stage has helped further deepen my understanding of, appreciation for, and love of the craft.

I still experience nerves occasionally, but instead of seeing these as a sign that I'm not good enough, I now understand these are symptoms of my passion. The butterflies in my stomach tell me I have something to share that I care deeply about. They're a sign of my excitement of what's to come for the audience once they realise that they too can dream bigger and achieve more of their life goals – even if they feel shy – knowing that every journey is different, and every dream is possible.

CHAPTER 10

Daydreams Do Come True

By Mila Johansen

From poverty to abundance, from hungry child to organic farmer, from daydreams to success. The small child who didn't pay attention in school, against all odds, became a successful writer, teacher, and public speaker.

Everything that happened to me built my character. Many of the events that took place in my life as a child became the cornerstones of who I have become today. The "Cinderella" in our household growing up, I did all the housework in our home, about four hours a day, from the age of ten.

I often went to school without lunch and watched all the kids sitting before me feast on packed lunches. I grew up in a very meagre, poor home with a single mother who was a third-grade teacher, which is part of the reason I'm a teacher today. She would leave at six in the morning and drive forty minutes to set up her classroom for her teaching job. So, I, at a very young age, had to get my brother up, make sure he got breakfast, and move us both out the door to walk a mile to school. Bobby was two and a half years younger than me. When we were very young, we often went to bed without dinner. Now I appreciate every single thing that is given to me.

I was a "glass half-full" kind of girl from the beginning. The very first movie I saw in a theatre was *Pollyanna* at the age of seven. That one movie affected me in so many ways. For one thing, I came home wishing there was a big screen on my bedroom wall so that I could watch Pollyanna any time I wanted. We didn't have a television in our home yet. I hadn't seen any other movie, except every Sunday night, we went across the street to my grandmother's house to watch Disney's *Sunday Night Movies*. I think it's amazing that we can watch anything we want anytime. I often still marvel at that.

So, my life has been a lot like the "Pollyanna" attitude in the movie—the "Glad Game." At one point, she tells the story of a time with her father. Pollyanna wanted a doll, so her father said, "Let's look in the church donation barrel." The only item they found that day was a pair of crutches. So, he said, "Let's play the Glad Game. Let's think of something to be glad for about finding the crutches." Pollyanna thought for a minute and then said, "Well, I guess I can be glad I don't need the crutches."

And that has always been my attitude with so many things. I'm not afraid to admit that I am a real life Pollyanna. For some reason, I've always thought I could have everything. I just had a feeling that my life was great, and nothing seemed to get me down. Maybe I often went hungry, but I always remained positive.

I want to tell you about a fantastic experience I had. . . I must have been a "glass half-full" girl even back then. I didn't realise I practised manifesting even in those days.

We drove to church every Sunday, and on the way, next to the freeway, there was an A-frame house. It was like a cabin, but big, with two stories. I loved it, and I thought, *I want that house*. I was eight. I wanted to live in that house. So, I started daydreaming about how I could get it. I thought I could somehow make the money I needed to buy it. Even at eight years old, I could have that house. Of course, I didn't get the house . . .then.

I asked my mother to stop one Sunday, and we went on a tour inside. A big sign we could read from the freeway was "Open House". So, we went in and looked around. I continued daydreaming that I could somehow have that house someday.

Around the same time, at age eight or nine, I wanted to be a writer. I wanted to be a writer more than I wanted to be anything else. We went to see *Mary Poppins*, another one of the first movies I ever went to; there weren't a lot of movies back then. We finally had a T.V., one of those old-fashioned brown boxes, furniture-looking things, with about three channels.

When I came home from the movie, I went into my bedroom, shut the door, and secretly made some chalk drawings—as I had seen in the movie. I closed my eyes and tried to jump in. I believed I could jump into the chalk drawings and be transported to a beautiful, magical world full of greenery, flowers, merry-go-rounds, and penguins. It didn't work. I tried at least five times. They were probably pitiful drawings because I've never been an artist and managed more than poorly drawn stick figures.

So, I thought I could be a writer and create magic that way. I loved to read *Nancy Drew* and *The Bobbsey Twins*. My mother read all fourteen of the OZ books by Frank Baum to me.

She had the entire set of hardbound volumes from her childhood in England. Later I read them all to myself.

I started writing a book the same day I made the chalk drawings. I wrote a page and a half and quit—because I was eight. But I knew then that I wanted to be a writer. Later in life, when I became a playwright, I wrote the first three OZ books into stunning musicals performed on many community theatre stages.

At age 18, my mother tricked me into becoming a writer. She said, "Mila, I know you have always wanted to be a writer, so why don't you write just one sentence daily for a month."

I agreed, thinking that I could stick to writing one sentence a day. But, it turned out, I couldn't just write one sentence. It's like potato chips, I found myself writing a page or two or more, and by the end of the month—I was a writer. Voila!

I always daydreamed. I don't think teachers liked me because my head lived in the clouds. I could never pay attention. I remember looking out the windows at the clouds marching by, imagining myself dancing on top of them.

Now I realise I spent my school days daydreaming about my future life. I spent those years sharpening my imagination and learning exactly what I needed for my future life as a writer.

I even started daydreaming about the man I was destined to meet. I started speaking to the stars—to the man I knew I would eventually marry. I lay in the curve of a large dolphin statue in a nearby park, looked up into the Milky Way Galaxy, and spoke out loud. I knew he waited out there for me. I knew him as if I had already met him.

I kept speaking to him, and when I went to four-year college, I met him in the most extraordinary way. We had each joined the same intramural coed baseball team that a mutual friend had put together. I showed up for the season's very first game, and no one came but one person, Rich. We had never met before that day and started talking. I knew I wanted to be part of his life within five minutes.

We finally had to officially forfeit the game since only two of us showed up. We shrugged and began walking in different directions: me towards home, and he headed towards the campus buildings. I suddenly turned around, caught up to him, and said, "Where are you going?" He said he wanted to work on his painting in the art department. I went along to see his work.

I told him I had a weekly dancing date that night with my girlfriend and asked if he wanted to meet me there. He did, and we started dating. He courted me by dropping off boxes of oranges on my doorstep. Later, I married him. He's an organic farmer, so I never went hungry again. We've been married for forty-three years now—one of the main abundances of my life. By the way, the rest of the team showed up to every other game after that fateful day.

When I met my husband, Rich, he put me to work on his family's organic citrus ranch. Lucky for him, he got a "Cinderella" because I had done that four hours a day of work at my house growing up. My brother only did a half hour a week—taking out the trash and mowing the tiny tract home lawn, which ruined him. He didn't make it out of our neighbourhood. He ended up being a casualty of our childhood in "gangland." I'm certain I survived because I became a worker and partly due to my extreme naivety.

So, when I got to the citrus ranch, I didn't mind doing all the work. When I saw all the fruit, the number twos (substandard for selling), I said, "Rich, there's so much extra fruit, we've got to give it away."

He said, "No, no, no, Mila. We don't give anything away." Rich is the most generous person I know, but his family came out of the Depression era and lived in that consciousness, even though they earned very good money, owning several businesses.

I insisted, "Oh yeah, we'll give it away." In the long run, I won out, and now we give 10,000 to 20,000 pounds a year to local food banks.

My grandmother was my Fairy Godmother. I spent much of my childhood listening to entertaining stories of her childhood and later adventures. Jessie Haver Butler, a famous suffragette, who became the first woman lobbyist at the Capitol in Washington D.C., came from a tragic childhood on a Colorado cattle ranch. (When I compare my childhood with hers, I count mine as a blessing.)

A teacher saw how bright Jessie was and helped her get into Smith College in New England, where she thrived. In her first job after graduating from Smith, she helped Professor Cunliffe put together the Pulitzer School of Journalism at Columbia. In her second job, she helped set the first minimum wage in the country for women, from $4.00 a week to $8.00; and worked hard to get children out of the factories.

In Washington D.C., she became the first official woman lobbyist and worked closely with Alice Paul and Carrie Chapman Catt to help women win the right to vote in 1920.

She later spoke all over London with George Bernard Shaw and taught Eleanor Roosevelt to speak. For some reason, she was destined to be on the front lines and part of many historical events. In her early nineties, she shared the podium several times with Gloria Steinem and Marlo Thomas and took me along. She half-raised me, which is why I turned out the way I had. Jessie and I were always together, joined at the heart.

To inspire us all, she made her last speech in Hollywood at age 94, then let her secretary go and passed away at 98. Jessie mastered reinventing herself through regular walking, swimming, and vitamins until the end. Because of knowing her, I've always said, even at eighteen, "I'm going to make a great old lady because I'm already eccentric." Jessie is the perfect example that it doesn't matter where we come from or what has happened to us; we can raise ourselves up and become anything.

Even though I grew up in poverty, I always had a generous heart. If one of my friends liked my blouse, I'd give it to her; I could get another one at the thrift store. I always feel that the more I give—which is one of my secrets—the more I get. But that's not why I do it. Giving seems like a puzzle to me, especially when no one knows about it. I treat it like a game to see how much I can give without getting caught. Besides, the more you give, the more you receive. There's enough for everyone—we must tap into the funnel to send it our way.

In my younger years, my consciousness scored low on the money scale. I didn't think I could have a lot of money at that point; I felt like I didn't deserve it. I've met many other people who have felt the same way. I've worked hard for every penny I've earned. We scrimped and saved for years. I remember never having more than a dollar in my pocket.

Then Rich and I started visiting La Jolla, in Southern California, to stay with part of his family who lived in the hills above the opulent town. They weren't particularly wealthy. After about three years of walking through the streets of La Jolla every summer, I started realising, "Wow, I could have some of this; this is for everybody." I started feeling that I belonged there. Even though I often came straight from boogie boarding in the ocean and went to La Jolla dressed in my ragged shorts, flip-flops, and a tunic.

I'd walk through the stores where owners weren't particularly happy to see me because I probably didn't buy anything. I just felt like it raised my consciousness that I would have money someday; I started getting that into my head and thinking about it and asking for it in my meagre way, though I've learned better ways now to do it.

I kept daydreaming—that's the most important thing. I had to visualize new things. I daydreamed about becoming a published writer. Another technique I started using was writing down lists of things I wished for and wanted to happen. Someone shared that technique with me, so I did it. I made my first list, which involved directing plays, writing books, and making more money.

It also had some basics, like flossing more and eating healthier. I wanted to be a published author. I wanted to teach classes. I had some impossible things in there, too. Two years later, in my late twenties, I looked at that list, and everything had come true.

So now I'm making new lists. And every time I make a list, when I go back to it—maybe even ten years later—all of it has come to fruition. Sometimes, the things you dream of and wish for don't come true immediately. They come true when you need them. I didn't realise I was manifesting all through my life—starting with not paying attention in grade school.

One important thing I did learn was in high school during my senior year. I mastered finger placement and typing. A very good thing for a writer. It's practically the only thing I learned because it was kinesthetic, and I'm a kinesthetic learner. I believe everyone should have to learn finger placement. I can't believe how many people I know who don't have that skill.

Then I started manifesting in a big way! I became a landscaper/gardener for a few years in addition to working on the citrus ranch. At the same time, I taught dance, a lot of dance. And I started teaching kids. I began teaching an after-school theatre program. I became a kind of "Jill" of all trades. These days, everyone is spouting, "Multiple streams of income." That's precisely what I did way back then. Now I give talks on how to create and juggle "multiple streams of income."

During landscaping jobs, I began daydreaming about how much money I wanted to make. I remember the exact amount—$500 a day. That became my goal. I couldn't believe it, but in two or three years, I brought in $500 a day through my ranch work and sales, combined with other endeavours. That turned out to be a huge amount back then. So, it came true. But I first said, "I'm going to do it," and believed in it. I've experienced many manifestations, but that was one of my first big, concentrated manifestations.

Remember that A-frame house? Recently, in the last eight years, my father-in-law needed to move in with us. We had always lived with him on the citrus ranch during harvests, and we knew we loved him and lived well together. At ninety years of age, he offered to help us build a house on our smaller farm in the foothills so he could move in. We built a big home near Nevada City in the foothills above Sacramento, California.

One day I went down to pick lavender below our new home. I looked back up at the house, which I had never done before. I couldn't believe it! The house was the A-frame house from my childhood, but three times as big—exactly the same house. I realised I had manifested it, but it took decades to happen. That turned out to be funny, profound, and a significant abundance in my life.

Daydreams hold a fantastic amount of power. One day, I looked back and realised that every single daydream I'd imagined had come true. I realised I needed to start remembering to dream new daydreams, to keep manifesting and creating the future.

CHAPTER 11

The Verbose Reticent Raconteur

By Rita Preston

I am not a public speaker. I am shy. I talk a lot. Ask my big sister; I never shut up! Ask close friends; I never shut up! Ask others; I hold my tongue and guard my words. Ask those who know me; I am extremely verbose! I love words!

I am slightly panicked as I sit here, attempting to write a chapter for a marvellous collaborative book. What am I doing? I am NOT a public speaker!

I strive not to speak in public. I experience severe stage fright! I detest speaking in public. I fear giggles if my voice cracks, or I lose my place if I falter. Hours before speaking, I may spend innumerable visits to 'the little room' as my body rebels against this task I've accepted.

Such things have haunted my physical form since my college days.

Presentations and speeches were many.

The biggest university reading before a crowd of 700+ yielded few nervous side effects. Odd.

Classrooms of 35 or fewer, and I was taking anti-diarrheal medications! Oddly, I received compliments galore for my large crowd reading.

I remained baffled at this human body that I inhabit.

I know when I began to be fearful of public performances.

I loved to play the clarinet and sing in primary school. I informed my music teacher that I wanted to participate in chorus and band when I enrolled at the middle school level.

I arrived at junior high school with plans, hopes, and dreams. I loved the band! I attended the choral practices for the first few days. The choral director asked each student to stand next to the piano while he played scales and such for us to sing back to him, acapella. I had not sung acapella since the youth chorus at church when that director said I had an amazing range.

I remember singing a few solos in the youth choir at church when still in primary school. Sometimes the director had me fill in if one of the boys was absent.

Suddenly, the middle-school chorus room seemed deafeningly silent. I opened my mouth and began the notes. I fell off key. I heard giggles, their sound enhanced by the silence of the room. I felt the flush of redness flashing from somewhere in my torso up through my neck to my face and ears. Even my hair felt as if it were on fire. Our patient director played the notes again to allow me to recover.

Everything was off-key then. More giggles from amidst the room.

Students at that early teen age do not have the worldly life experience to know not to giggle when someone makes a mistake. They are still learning, but it feels horribly cruel to the recipient. Sadly, too many today feel encouraged and take it to the extreme of bullying.

Thankfully, my experience did not involve meanness; it was simply horribly embarrassing but went no further.

The next class day, the choir had been removed from my schedule.

I silently vowed to myself never to be heard singing in public again. I sang in my bedroom with the music emanating from my record player (something popular from the 1950s to the early 1980s).

I sang in the car while alone once I passed my driving test. I sang in my college dormitory room when my roommate was absent. I sang in a summer missionary choir for one week every summer (escaping solo).

I still sing in my car, even with the windows down! I sing loudly, sometimes off-key, but I sing! I love low notes. I loved low notes in the high school band, switching from a B-flat clarinet to an alto clarinet and eventually to a contra-bass clarinet.

Fondly, there are recollections of my big sister telling someone how she loved when we were all in church and hearing our family singing in the back pews: my hubby singing base, my youngest stepson singing tenor, her singing alto and me singing soprano.

I thought that was silly. They could sing, but I was no vocalist.

How did I let a few giggles and some flat notes shut my public voice?

Middle school / junior high school early-pre-teen years are difficult for anyone. Hormones, new schools, life changes, all these things affect us in those years.

We develop new habits, new neurosis, and new tastes. We learn about making best friends, enemies, bullies, and mere acquaintances. We develop our first crushes and are overwhelmed with the inundation of the world around us. Life changes after primary school.

Today's society in the 21st century is dramatically different than it was for those growing up in the late 20th century and even more different than those growing up in prior centuries.

The Industrial Revolution of the mid-1700s through the mid-late 1800s dramatically changed our world. It provided opportunities that previously had not existed for the everyday working person.

It permitted women to build their collective voice in societies across the globe. (Sadly, some cultures have not accepted that advancement.)

As the industry advanced, so, too, did technology. With technology, the advanced cultures on the planet have leapt forward, supposedly finding 'better ways to accomplish things.' Our global connections have increased, our world seems smaller, and we are more connected than ever. We can have live 'in-person' chats, videos, seminars, and giant presentations, all through the internet and video connections.

These would amaze our ancestors from a mere 300 years ago!

With all these technological inventions, our public speaking venues have changed. Children may still give presentations on the take-your-parent-to-work day. University students still present their speeches and doctoral thesis to faculty in lecture halls. Corporations manage global conference calls on large screens and stereo surround-sound speakers. Students are learning to adapt to video calls with each passing day.

Public speaking is no longer just walking on stage in front of 35 listeners in a small church, but to thousands in a stadium.

Speakers and big screens make us more hearable, visible, and relatable. Those same presentations are live-streamed via social media and other video channels. Sometimes there is no live audience. (I am reminded of the old days of live television when 'canned laughter' became a known 'thing' in media.)

I have not been called on frequently as an adult to speak publicly, but I find myself willing, even if reluctant. I still feel my nerves rebelling.

There may be another trip to the pharmacy to pick up some relief for my symptoms.

I drink more water to stay hydrated and keep my skin healthier. That helps.

There was a time when I directed Vacation Bible School at our church for several years. Part of my job was to speak at the opening program every day. I dreaded that. (You can read more about that in MO2VATE Magazine's "Sole Inspiration" article.)

I loved it. I was encouraged by the receptive, eager looks on the children's faces and our volunteers. The do-or-die day came when I had nothing for the opening one night. God provided, and I felt joy as I shared with the students about my red shoes. I could speak in public! There was joy in my soul!

Holding the attention of an audience takes a lot of work.

Sitting in many seminars during my 32-year profession of income taxes taught me to avoid eating heavy lunches and not sit up front after lunch! Monotone speakers will induce afternoon naps!

I love to laugh and have learned to hold a conversation if I can share a funny true story, something to which the listener can relate. I love to hear others laugh. If I can make a sour person smirk, I consider it a good day.

I joke with many that someday when I grow up, I want to be a comedienne, the President, or maybe both! (Some say that's the same thing, but that's an entirely separate topic.)

Laughter is good for the soul, the psyche, the human existence – however you want to describe it.

No matter how serious or dry the topic to be presented, you, the speaker, can find mechanisms to keep the discourse light. Surely, you need to cover the serious details, but you can catch your breath, vary your speaking tone, and allow the audience to find the brilliance of the topic so that they do not doze off.

As a side note, and perhaps needing a study, which is more embarrassing: falling asleep in a live seminar in person or nodding off without shutting off your live video on a Zoom conference? Food for thought!

None of us wants to bore our listeners to death. If we bore them repeatedly, they will tune out permanently. How do we keep them engaged? How do we keep them coming back for more?

If you have students required to listen to you for course credit, you, as a speaker, have it made.

Those students, those listeners, are your prisoners, and you can bore them in a monotone all you want. They will listen, try to stay awake, and take notes. The catch is when they can pick you for an elective course in the future, will they sign up? Probably not.

As a speaker, you want to engage your students, audience, and listeners so that they keep returning for more. You want to be hired to speak repeatedly. You want your podcast to be picked up by more networks. The more you sell yourself, the more revenue you generate too. It isn't all about ego; sometimes, you want to make a living!

Herein lies the big question as a speaker, what do you have to say that people want to hear?

Look at the markets out there. Are you an expert in a specific genre?

Are you a financial wizard?

Are you extra sharp in early childhood education?

Are you an advocate for veterans?

Do you like to tell jokes?

Are you a superb operatic performer?

I once attended a convention wherein the guest speaker/entertainer was a professional musician who incorporated his musical talents into this speech about inspiring others to their fullest potential. It was phenomenal! I never felt the urge to look at my watch once during the entire 1.5-hour presentation!

When you step up on the stage (whether it's a boulder in a national park or a 100' stage in an arena), who do you see in front of you? Do you see "us" or "them"?

I used to see them. A friend told me, "But it's just us in the congregation." I pointed out that we were us until I climbed the few steps to the platform, and the rest became "them".

Until that night at Vacation Bible School, the audience was always 'them.'

I am still working on the us/them syndrome. I have come to accept that we are all 'us'. Truly. We are all human beings. We are all born the same, and we shall all leave this life in similar manners. We are unique, but we are still human.

We choose to connect or step away from each other. The older I get, the more I realise that those connections are essential for the betterment of humankind.

It is perfectly fine to prefer time alone and exist independently, but we also need good human interaction over decades. Whether attempting to impart new mathematical concepts or trying to entertain by promoting our latest artwork, we need human connection.

Will I get nervous the next time I am asked to give a presentation?

You bet.

Will I get nervous if I am called upon to speak about any given topic? Absolutely.

Will I turn down speaking opportunities? Now and then.

Will I accept speaking engagements? Absolutely, depending on the topic.

I will not speak 'for' a topic that goes against my personal beliefs. I will debate the opposing viewpoint, but I will not promote it. (To me, that is tantamount to false advertising).

I will force myself to find a way to speak on certain topics dear to my heart: veterans' needs, children's rights, cancer awareness, domestic violence, community involvement, and a few others.

I may still feel my hands tremble (thankful for podiums to grip), feel as though I ate a bag of cotton balls, and even regret accepting the opportunity, but I will do it.

I have said more than once that I will gladly make a fool of myself for children. I will do that for a few others too.

I am not ready to sing a public solo yet, but I am willing to speak.

I will share your words if you are too frightened but need your words heard. I will be your voice. If you are afraid to ask, whisper. Send an email. Shoot a text.

I will advocate for you when you cannot.

I have a calling in my heart that I cannot explain, to take up torches for those who cannot do so themselves.

I may make myself a nervous wreck in the process, but there have been times when I felt I had no voice. (I experienced a stalking situation years ago; again, another story.)

There was a time when I felt I could not pray. A wise friend was led to intercessory prayer for whom she did not know. She heard of my plight, hugged me, and said calmly, "Now I know for whom I am to be praying."

Sometimes we need an intercessor, whether in prayer, speaking, or at our daily job. We all need helping hands. We need to be willing to ask. We need to be willing to answer the call.

I still fear my voice falling flat. I fear blushing. I fear giggles. I also relish giggles when I purposely cause them. I have a voice given to me by God, and I shall use it the best that I can.

You may wish I would shut up some days, but I will not be silenced. I shall speak, share, and ramble!

My words, however diverse, have a purpose. I may not always know the purpose, but my words spill forth!

I still say stupid things. I forget to watch my volume. I am human. I am a work in progress.

All I ask is that you don't throw things at me! Give me constructive criticism so that I may do better. Don't giggle unless it's funny. Guffaw if it is decidedly humorous.

I have much to learn, but my voice has value; so does yours.

It is OK to be nervous. You are human with a voice to be heard.

CHAPTER 12

Speaking as a Necessity

By Sharon Brown

My story may be a little different to others in this book, as my ambition isn't to become a professional public speaker. I've never aspired to do this, however being in the profession I work in, it is a necessity.

As a child and young adult, I was extremely shy. It's hard to believe I was the same person as now. I always speak up for myself and like to think of myself as an 'activist' because I stick up for the underdog, and I hate seeing injustice in any form. I've walked out of jobs because of the unfairness I've witnessed and told Managers exactly how I feel. In these circumstances, my shyness disappears. I'd go as far as to say, it's a total turnaround and sometimes I say too much!

I'm very much the same in my business. I have a friendly demeanour which many have mistaken for being weak or soft. Lines have been crossed, and my friendly demeanour changes, much to the surprise of the offending party. So, I'm not sure where my shyness originated from, although I guess it's maybe from my Dad. My mum is an extrovert and always has been, so I have a bit of both.

When I was singled out in class or anywhere, the shyness would kick in, and I would turn a rosy red colour and clam up! I'm not even sure when this changed and at what age, but I'm guessing probably when I started my own business eight years ago, although I did have some experiences working in corporate that forced me to stand up and talk out in public.

The first notable experience where I felt the ground should swallow me up was when I was assisting with the Farmers Weekly Awards for our Dairy Sector. I had to attend an event at a beautiful venue as an introduction to the team and to learn about what was planned that year. I remember sitting there when the host asked everyone to stand up and introduce themselves, I could have run out of that room at full speed at that very moment. The closer it came to me standing up, my throat was drying, the anxiety was kicking in, and the sense of panic was beginning to take hold. I kept trying to tell myself that it was crazy what I was feeling and to breathe…. The moment came and went in less than 10 seconds, but I can honestly say it was horrible. I'm not sure if it was me speaking or all the eyes on me that were worse.

I moved to the West Midlands from Scotland in 2003, and since then, I have always been very aware of my accent. Back home, I felt more comfortable in my skin and just blended in with the native speakers. In England, I was acutely aware my accent stood out, which meant I stood out. This is a lot for someone who is naturally shy and it didn't feel good for me at that time.

Over the years, my accent has changed a little. It's more rounded, although everyone can still tell I'm Scottish (which I'm happy about). I feel far more confident now being that centre of attention as I've had to adjust running my business.

The game-changing moment for me came in the same corporate position as above; I had to address the whole events team and volunteers and provide a 30-minute presentation on our annual Livestock Event, the biggest one on the calendar each year. I was seconded to this Project Manager position with a huge responsibility as the show always had a massive footfall with thousands of visitors yearly. Still, I knew I was damn good at the job as I'd always organised events and knew my energy, enthusiasm, and experience would consistently deliver.

The day came, and the same feelings of anxiety started rising. The time was closing in, and I was trying to feel relaxed, not build it up too much in my head; knowing I had prepared for hours the day prior helped a little.

Everyone started to pile in as we entered the room with a U shape layout, with me at the helm. The seats were taken, and many people were standing, waiting for the presentation to start. I didn't realise then that they were filming it too to send to the remote workers helping at the event...'gulp'!

I took a breath and began. My voice held steady, although I'm sure I was bright red when I started the introduction. However, surprisingly, I started leaning into it ten minutes in. Could this be happening? I asked myself. I was relaxing and feeling more confident.

When it ended, I received a round of applause. Many of the staff knew how nervous I had been and this was a big deal for me at the time.

I watched the footage back and surprised myself. I was coherent and calm and came across really well, better than I had expected. I wasn't the quivering mess I thought or felt at the time. Somehow, I had managed to keep it together and get the points across that were needed.

Afterwards, I felt great. Not because I think I did a fantastic job, but more that I just did it, whatever the outcome was... I faced my fear, stood outside of my comfort zone and did what I needed to do. That in itself was a significant win for me that day. It may seem small to some people, but when it's a personal achievement, it's like winning the lottery.

After starting my business in 2015, I knew I would need to get over my fears in this area. I started an Events Agency, so the chances of me having to host events was highly likely. This was the case as I started in the live music area, so I had to get on stage and introduce acts, thank audiences etc., and I certainly embraced these opportunities.

My business has completely changed now, but I still host small events across my platforms, both online and F2F.

I enjoy the experience now as it's never too serious, and usually like chatting with a group of friends.

The fears that raise their ugly heads, discussed in this book, are things like, what if I freeze? What if I talk rubbish or ramble on? What if I bore people? These are all fears that are normal and that everyone goes through. Even seasoned speakers, singers, and comedians get stage fright and have the same insecurities. The difference is in facing them. Some people will never choose to put themselves in that situation, whereby others will! Stepping outside that comfort zone is always challenging, as staying precisely where we feel safe and nice is far easier.

However, the feeling of pure elation after you have faced your fear is quite addictive. Practice makes perfect, as they say, and the more you keep doing something, the better and more comfortable you will become at it. Rome wasn't built in a day, so don't expect too much from yourself initially. Mistakes will always be part of your journey. Embrace them and learn from them.

Nowadays, I enjoy hosting events. I enjoy bringing my sense of humour, asking questions and anything else I choose to speak about. If asked to be a compere, I'd probably accept the challenge now as I feel confident in myself as a business owner and to know that actually I can do a great job at this with preparation.

Is public speaking something I want to do as an add-on to my business? The answer is still NO... why? Because I enjoy doing other things, is the simple answer.

Do I speak when I need to? YES, because it's my job, and I don't shy away from things now.

My future business plans will require me to speak to large audiences, but it doesn't fill me with anxiety now. I know what I want from my future, and I know that this will be part of achieving that.

If you have anxiety with just the thought of standing up and speaking in front of an audience, here are some things I've learned that hopefully will reduce that fear for you:

1. You've heard of the book, 'Feel the Fear, but do it anyway'? This is so true. It may feel like the most challenging thing at that moment, but concentrate on how you'll feel afterwards. That's what I did. I kept saying it's only 10 minutes, or only half an

hour out of my life, then It's over, and it hasn't beat me. Putting it into a time bracket helped me and seemed like a very small ask in the big scheme of things!

2. Preparing will always make you feel more confident. This is for everything in life. You wouldn't run a marathon unless you had prepared, would you? It's no different for presentations or speaking. Prepare your lines; know your beginning, middle and end and what message you're trying to get across. Practise it over and over until you know you sound good. Do it in the mirror. It might make you cringe at first, but then you'll get a feel for how others perceive you, and your confidence will soar.

3. If you're a business owner, think of speaking as another arm of your business. It's something that will be required of you. You speak daily to people at networking events or online, so why should this be any different? You will shine if you know your topic, especially if you're passionate about it. People can always tell when you're passionate with purpose and freely give information.

4. When you feel that anxiety and panic... try not to run away; face it head-on and take deep breaths. Lean into the challenge and be clear that the outcome doesn't matter as you're doing it anyway.

5. Watch others. A great way of learning to improve is to watch how others are doing it and succeeding at it. How are they engaging the audience? What are they doing to get people interacting? What is their secret sauce? Then talk to some audience members and ask what they liked about various speakers. You can then practise some of these tactics on your own.

Public speaking will be like marmite. You'll either love it or hate it. If it's the latter, learn at least to accept it as part of your business model. You don't have to go onto massive stages, but you will likely want to run a workshop, a book launch, a networking event or an event of some kind at some point. Or you will be asked to talk about your chosen subject. Either way, be ready to say YES. Not only does this give your brand a boost, but it exposes your business to others, which can and is only a good thing. Vulnerability can be very powerful when relating to others, so embrace your insecurities. You could even share your story with the audience which will definitely resonate with some.

The last part of my story is a contradiction. I started The Speakers Index, which is a public speakers directory and magazine, based on the fact that I am not a major fan of public speaking. I know I'm not alone, and there are many people who run businesses out there, just like me.

I wanted to start something that helped them get exposure to the opportunities that might change their lives and help them grow in this area…

So, if you have leaned into your public speaking and would like to be part of a small community of speakers who share their stories in this book, get in touch!

sharon@thespeakersindex.com

CHAPTER 13

Permission to Speak

By Tabby Kerwin

In my early years, performing came naturally to me. I was trained to perform as a musician, on stage and as a dancer, not necessarily because it was my desire to, but because it was expected of me.

Being a performer was a pathway I was set on as a young child, and I was comfortable with it and very fortunate and grateful for the opportunities it has brought me throughout my life. Performing was about applying a persona to myself in order to entertain others, and it gave me the confidence to stand in front of others and deliver.

The truth is that for many years my performance wasn't my authentic voice but the words and music written by others which I had developed the confidence to deliver with ease, memorising the details to appease and please my audience.

It was a mask... a mask that I wore from childhood into adult life, not just to perform, but to survive. That mask gave me my power to perform publicly whilst being my protection from the real world.

What the mask was doing was covering my developing social anxiety and depression.

For around 10 years in my 20s and 30s, I lived with depression and social anxiety, born out of living with childhood grief and a lack of self-compassion, self-confidence and fear of the judgements of others. It was a surreal decade in that I could stand and perform publicly with zero fears as a professionally trained musician, yet stood in a circle of colleagues or friends I could feel myself in emotional and physical turmoil.

Despite having people around me, it was a grey, numb and lonely time, and I kept my mask on the whole time. Even those close to me did not know the pain and anguish I was feeling and living with – because publicly, I was still performing and functioning and doing what was expected as a professional, a wife and a mother.

In 2010 I hit my lowest moment – a fleeting moment when suicidal thoughts came into my head - and on sharing that truth I was dismissed; met with a laugh and a change of subject.

THAT was THE moment.

The moment I knew everything had to change because I knew I could be happier. The moment I knew I deserved more and the moment I knew I had to change it. Change became a MUST in order to live.

My pathway to recovery commenced… a lifelong path to - as I termed it - #createmyhappy. I knew it was possible to be happier, so I committed to putting the work in to change from the inside out and, most importantly, to find my authentic voice.

As I changed my lifestyle, my relationships with myself and others and opened up to the possibility of change through my philosophy of the Three Ps: possibility, productivity and performance, I began to think, see and act more clearly and over the following years my confidence to be my true self developed.

When I performed now, it was authentic. I gave myself permission to speak my truth and share my story in open, honest conversations, both privately and publicly. Out of my years of struggle and adversity, I became visible.

The more I spoke, the more people would contact me and say how much my story resonated with them, and that gave me a drive, focus and permission to share even more and share consistently.

My message became that whatever you are going through or have been through, whatever hardship or barrier life throws at you, it is possible to create your own happiness.

The only caveat? YOU have to put in the work yourself. No one can do it for you.

From this point onwards, when I performed, there was no mask. It was my true, authentic and happy self speaking and sharing.

The permission I gave myself in those early days was huge, and sharing my story and philosophy through books and speaking opportunities was hugely important. Those opportunities also allowed me to become even stronger, for which I was grateful because, having already embraced the death of my brother after years of mental illness in 2014, my biggest test was to come. Would I have the emotional capacity to manage this life-changing event?

In 2018 after a short illness, my amazing husband, best friend, lover and business partner Simon died. Simon had been my constant through my darkest years, and we were both so happy to have upgraded our friendship to marriage in 2016 when the opportunity presented itself.

I had lived with this belief that I had found my strength and happiness because I had Simon, my biggest cheerleader, my strength and support. What I came to learn when he died was that I had not started to flourish because he was with me by my side but because he had equipped me with the tools to be mentally healthy and perform at my best, personally and professionally.

When Simon died, I had a choice. A choice to be overwhelmed as a widow, mum and business owner or a choice to flourish. I opted for the latter. I took the window of opportunity you are given when grieving, which allows you to be your authentic self, feeling all your emotions, and I took that permission granted by others, and I ran with it.

Where was I running to? Towards visibility. Towards a place where I could help myself and others heal, flourish, be emotionally fitter and PERFORM at their best, sharing stories and their unique, authentic voices.

It was time to really speak up… the journey was truly taking off.

I have a passion for sharing my lived and personal experiences to help and support others, and if my story resonates and I can help just one person through my written or spoken word, then every word I say is worth it for me.

The opportunity to speak, write, and share my authentic voice and experience is a privilege… and I choose to speak about taboo subjects.

In particular, The Three Taboos; Cancer, grief and mental health (the title of my second book) - all things I have experienced, either because I lived with them or lost from them. My Dad died when I was 16 years old of cancer, and Simon's short illness, which he was being treated for a cure, and which treatment kicked its backside (he just got caught out on a treatment technicality), was a germ cell tumour; a form of testicular cancer.

Speaking openly about taboo subjects sits uncomfortably with many people, but that resistance and discomfort experienced by some make me even more driven to bring difficult conversations to the table and speak about them openly, bravely and honestly.

Everyone will experience emotional distress, and a high percentage of people will experience poor mental health, with many developing mental illnesses. We will all experience grief at some point in our lives – loss is inevitable whether it is a loss of a person, pet, job or lifestyle and suicide is way too common globally but also one of the most preventable deaths if only we would start the open conversations about it and stop hiding out of fear and shame. Plus, 1 in 2 of us will be touched by cancer, a heart-breaking illness that is not proud or selective about who it visits.

These seemingly taboo subjects need to be discussed, however uncomfortable they may feel and however resistant people may be to talk about them.

By finding my voice, giving myself permission to speak authentically and becoming visible, I intend to help others have hope, see the possibility of a flourishing life even when life seems hard and know that they are not alone. I am here to walk through the experience with them through the comfort of my words, shared from my lived and professional experience.

I am an inherent learner and always curious to grow and learn more, allowing me to speak confidently. I constantly work to develop myself professionally, from training to be an instructor for Mental Health First Aid England and the

National Centre of Suicide Prevention and Training to completing my Masters in Applied Positive Psychology and on a personal level, I am committed to taking action to grow and flourish and constantly increase and maintain my emotional fitness to protect my mental health and PERFORM at my best.

As a child I would just perform... do what I was told and deliver. Now I authentically PERFORM, and it is a holistic experience that empowers me to share more, speak more and support others more as a consequence of others protecting their mental health and building their emotional fitness to have the capacity and resources to manage life when it challenges them.

I have created and developed The PERFORM Experience ® based on my authentic voice. It comprises the seven core pillars made up of; *Possibility, Enjoyment, Resilience, Focus, Optimism, Relationships and Mindset.*

When we align our energy with these seven pillars, we can not only see the possibility available for us, but we build our confidence to flourish... and it starts with self-compassion. Prioritise yourself to be your best for yourself and others.

You see, a huge part of my speakers' journey and sharing my authentic voice is about empowering others to find their voice; to find their love and compassion and strength from their own lived and professional experiences and to allow people to share their hardest moments bravely and courageously to heal, grow and contribute.

By sharing and speaking openly and honestly, we can also help reduce stigma around taboo subjects – if only we were to listen and communicate non-judgementally and fundamentally, that is part of my key message as a speaker.

As a breed, we are storytellers. Storytelling can be traced back to the earliest days through not just the written word but drawing, music and dance. We are creatives, and by telling our stories we understand more, we inspire more and we connect more.

Speaking allows us to connect, which is critical to protecting mental health. Often when people feel low and experience depression or anxiety, it comes from a sense of disconnection, be that from themselves, other people or the world around them. When we experience illness, grief or any hardship, we need the support and connection of others.

Equally, when life is amazing, we need to celebrate and connect through joy.

What I've learned through my experience of speaking publicly and privately is that by sharing our stories, we gain so much through the connections we make. We learn so much about ourselves, others and the world around us. We have the privilege of offering people hope, possibility and optimism, and we can inspire and motivate ourselves and others to PERFORM at our best.

My speakers' journey has been a rollercoaster of highs and lows. It's seen me navigate amazing opportunities and the biggest life-changing realities... but taking that initial permission slip from myself to share allowed me to experience a genuine heartfelt connection.

That's not to say it's always easy; no journey ever is, but it is more undulating than a mountainous journey these days. When you speak about seemingly taboo subjects, you open yourself to resistance, criticism and judgement. But I welcome those responses these days and view them as opportunities for deeper, more meaningful conversations with people who need them.

My social anxiety was born out of the fear of the judgement of others. That fear stopped me from sharing my authentic voice, even though my capacity for public performance was high, but once a wise friend told me that the opinions of others are not my concern, and that is true.

I can't control how or what people think. I can't control their opinions. But I can guide them towards staying out of judgement and learn from their thoughts to make my voice louder, become more visible and ultimately speak even louder.

Speaking about some of the most challenging and taboo subjects is a privilege. It is a privilege to have the opportunity and confidence to speak authentically. It is a privilege to support others, connect and help them find their authentic voice and, most importantly, to PERFORM at their best.

While I have been on this journey for several decades, it feels like my speakers' journey is just starting. I have so much to share and say, and as I learn more about myself, others and my areas of expertise, it empowers me to speak more and to speak louder. I have shared many stories with many people, and I have so many more stories to tell and stories to create through my future experiences.

My mask is lifted; I share the stories I want to speak about openly and honestly, and my original message is still at the core of what I do and believe. Whatever you are going through or have been through, whatever hardship or barrier life throws at you, it is possible to create your own happiness.

It is possible to thrive and flourish, learn and grow, but it does take action. It takes consistent daily work that we should invest in because every one of us is worthy of more, love, abundance, and sharing our own stories and speaking with our authentic voices without judgement.

Through my words, I hope to inspire others. I can motivate people to be more, want more and feel safer. I can empower them to invest in themselves to be emotionally fitter, protect their mental health and PERFORM at their best. I encourage them to move towards flourishing.

Mostly, if nothing else, I hope my speakers' journey shows people that it can be safe to lift their masks and by doing so, it offers them the opportunity to connect with the right people and share their own stories, which could well become the manual and guide for someone else to find the strength they need to raise their mask and speak their truth… and so forth.

We all have an authentic voice and should never feel we can't share it. By speaking our truth, we create pathways of possibility to flourishing and begin our exciting and unique journey.

My speakers' journey is one of pure privilege and joy and one I intend to keep on navigating for many years to come for the benefit of others and, of course, myself because I still have so much to learn and share and plan to. Will you be listening?

For more information on me and my creative portfolio, visit www.modefor.co.uk

EPILOGUE

Thank you for purchasing a copy of this book.

I hope you were able to find some answers to your own situation or take some knowledge away to use in your own life.

The Authors within these pages have dedicated their career to finding the answers on areas they are passionate about and are dedicated to sharing those life lessons with their audiences.

If you would like to share your own experience, please do contact us for details on how you can take part in our next book.

If you enjoyed this book, we would love a review on Amazon.

ABOUT THE CREATOR

SHARON BROWN moved to the West Midlands in 2003 from Glasgow in Scotland. In 2006, as a sideline, Sharon started the first Speed-dating business in the West Midlands at the height of its popularity, which ran for two successful years.

With a wide-ranging career in Event Management, Marketing, Project Management and board level support in various industries, Sharon started an Events Agency in 2015, now known as Lydian Group Ltd.

However, after realising that business was heading more towards the online digital space, Sharon left the Events Industry and launched four online platforms consecutively.

The first platform was a Women in Business online membership project namely, Revival Sanctuary, in 2018 with a mission of creating an environment of 'Collaboration over Competition'.

Two further projects were launched during lockdown (2020) with the aim of helping small business owners build their brands through speaking, writing, publishing, and collaborative working. MO2VATE Magazine was created in six weeks from concept to implementation and received a fantastic following through its subscribers and supporters. It's now had a complete facelift as MO2VATE Media, seeing it evolve as a membership driven business and information hub.

The Speakers Index was the third platform to be launched as Sharon saw a gap in the market around Speaking Agencies and the lack of promotion towards their speakers.

The Speakers Index is an online directory which also houses a quality Speakers Magazine highlighting the speakers' talents.

Members are encouraged to create a full profile giving all the information needed by an Organiser who can then contact them directly through their contact details on the website or in the magazine.

The Book Chief Publishing House is Sharon's latest project, launched in 2021 and already with an impressive resume of clients and Authors.

Sharon's vision was to provide an all-in-one affordable publishing service turning small business owners into credible authors through a robust and structured process. The Book Chief portfolio has exponentially grown during 2022 and continues to build huge momentum, onboarding clients mainly through referral marketing and retained Author portfolios.

SERVICES

MO2VATE MEDIA

(formerly MO2VATE Magazine)

MO2VATE Media is a global digital business hub covering topics across business industries, health, inspiration, lifestyle, politics, opinion / research-based information, entrepreneur insights and many other topics, founded by Sharon Brown.

All articles are written by business owners and the project is managed by independent entrepreneurs. The online hub runs yearly International Awards and produces various books written by the Contributors who are part of the MO2VATE community.

Mo2vatemedia.com

editor@mo2vatemagazine.com

THE BOOK CHIEF PUBLISHING

The Book Chief Publishing House was born during the latter end of the pandemic with a mission to support business owners and lovers of writing, on their path to becoming credible Authors.

The Book Chief publishes every age group, genre, type and size of book and advises on every step of producing Authors books from book covers, titles, book descriptions, and growing through the relevant rankings on Amazon and much more.

The Book Chief has a great track record in customer service and of producing great results for Authors books, in layout, editing, design and marketing.

As a one-stop shop for all Publishing needs, and payment plans to spread the cost, it should be the first stop for those looking to publish and spread the word about their book! Lots of additional services to choose from too!

Thebookchief.com

sharon@thebookchief.com

THE SPEAKERS INDEX

The Speakers Index is an online directory for speakers and event organisers designed to improve their chances of being seen by the right people.

We produce a quarterly magazine where each speaker features on a double page spread. The magazine is sent out through social media and to our email list on each publication.

Working similar to an agency but without any additional fees or commission, The Speakers Index also creates events to allow speakers to participate and be seen.

Thespeakersindex.com

sharon@thespeakersindex.com

REVIVAL SANCTUARY

Revival Sanctuary was the very first online platform founded by Sharon Brown in 2018, designed to create an environment of support, encouragement and celebration for women in business. With a mission to help women embrace a mindset of collaboration over competition, Revival created a beautiful safe space for women who join, to be completely themselves, without judgement.

The platform comprises a WhatsApp group for real time conversation and discussion. Quarterly meet-ups are organised in London with varying activities for the ladies to join in and just enjoy a great day connecting and having fun and online coffee chats happen monthly to allow overseas members to connect with anyone who joins in.

sharon@revivalsanctuary.co.uk

Printed in Great Britain
by Amazon

21844495R00116